The Role and Impact of Public-Private Partnerships in Education

Harry Anthony Patrinos
Felipe Barrera-Osorio
Juliana Guáqueta

THE WORLD BANK
Washington, D.C.

ISBN: 978-0-8213-7866-3
eISBN: 978-0-8213-7903-5
DOI: 10.1596/978-0-8213-7866-3

Library of Congress Cataloging-in-Publication Data
Patrinos, Harry Anthony.
    The role and impact of public-private partnerships in education / Harry Anthony Patrinos, Felipe Barrera-Osorio, and Juliana Guáqueta.
        p. cm.
    Includes bibliographical references and index.
    ISBN 978-0-8213-7866-3 (alk. paper) — ISBN 978-0-8213-7903-5
    1. Privatization in education.   2. Public-private sector cooperation.   I. Barrera-Osorio, Felipe.   II. Guáqueta, Juliana.   III. Title.
    LB2806.36.P39 2009
    379.1—dc22

                                                                                        2008054279

Cover art: Katerina Mertikas (www.katerinamertikas.com)
Cover design: Bill Pragluski, Critical Stages

The Role and Impact of Public-Private Partnerships in Education

Contents

Boxes

Figures

Tables

Foreword

Education is widely believed to be critical for any nation's economic, political, and social development. It is widely believed to help people escape from poverty and participate more fully in society and in the market place. These are a few of the reasons why governments around the world assume the responsibility for providing and financing education, especially basic education. But this responsibility is a large and complex one for any government to meet adequately, which is why it is important for governments to explore diverse ways of financing and providing educational services.

This book presents the results of the first phase of a multi-year program to examine the role of public-private partnerships in education. It focuses on contracting models at the primary and secondary education levels. It reviews the conceptual underpinnings for why such partnerships might contribute to achieving a country's education goals, reviews empirical evidence, and offers some guidelines for operations. The next phase of this agenda will focus on international and multi-stakeholder partnerships, including philanthropic initiatives on the one hand and for-profit activities on the other.

The book examines five ways through which public-private contracts can help countries meet education goals. First, public-private partnerships can increase access to good quality education for all, especially for poor children who live in remote, underserved communities and for children in minority populations. Second, lessons for innovative means of financing education can be particularly helpful in post-conflict countries undergoing reconstruction. Third, lessons about what works in terms of public-private partnerships contribute to the development of a more differentiated business model especially for middle-income countries. Fourth, the challenge of meeting the education Millennium Development Goals in less than a decade is a daunting one in the poorest countries. Understanding new partnership arrangements within a broad international aid architecture in education can help bring us closer to those goals. Fifth, some very innovative public-private partnership arrangements are happening in Arab countries, and lessons can be drawn from their experience.

Evidence is emerging from evaluations of the impact of projects funded by the World Bank, particularly with support from the Dutch government through the Bank-Netherlands Partnership Program (BNPP) Trust Fund. These evaluations are expanding knowledge about the benefits and the costs of these arrangements through rigorous analytical strategies and unique data from investment projects. In education, the BNPP is supporting evaluations in Kenya, Mexico, Pakistan, and the Philippines of initiatives aimed at reducing service provider absenteeism; giving financial and technical support to the expansion of private schooling for the poor; and funding school facilities, new education technologies, and parental participation. Although much is being learned from these ongoing evaluations, they are also raising more and deeper questions, helping policymakers and the development community to explore various ways to meet shared education goals.

Elizabeth M. King
Director, Education
Human Development Network
The World Bank

Acknowledgments

We acknowledge the significant contributions made by Juan-Diego Alonso, Shaista Baksh, Tazeen Fasih, John Fielden, Norman LaRocque, Michael Latham, Kevin Macdonald, Stefan Metzger, Emilio Porta, and Yidan Wang. Fiona J. Mackintosh and Bruce Ross-Larson provided excellent editing. The team received very useful feedback, guidance, and supervision from Ruth Kagia and Robin Horn.

The peer reviewers, Svava Bjarnason, April Harding, Juan Manuel Moreno, and Alberto Rodriguez, all gave excellent comments.

We received early feedback during an authors' workshop in May 2008 from Raja Bentaouet-Kattan, Erik Bloom, Marguerite Clarke, Ariel Fiszbein, Jay Kimmelman, Bruno Laporte, Joy Phumaphi, Periklis Saragiotis, and Emiliana Vegas. In addition, thoughtful comments were received at both the concept and final review stages from Helen Abadzi, Jacob Bregman, Samuel Carlson, Elizabeth King, Mamta Murthi, Halsey Rogers, Adriaan Verspoor, and Hana Yoshimoto.

The ongoing program on public-private partnerships is undertaken in collaboration with teams across the World Bank Group and with partners in developing countries. We are also collaborating with CfBT Education Trust, whose experts also work on this topic, and with the World Economic Forum's Global Education Initiative. In addition, we have an international steering committee of experts, comprising current and former country policymakers and representatives of multilateral organizations, such as the United Nations Educational, Scientific, and Cultural Organization (UNESCO).

Abbreviations

AVEC	Venezuelan Association of Catholic Schools
BRAC	Bangladesh Rural Advancement Committee
BTL	build-transfer-lease
CARE	Cooperation for Advancement, Rehabilitation, and Education
ESC	Educational Service Contracting (Philippines)
FAPE	Fund for Assistance to Private Education
FAS	Financial Assistance per Child Enrolled Basis Program (Pakistan)
ICFES	Instituto Colombiano para el Fomento de la Educación Superior
ICT	information and communication technology
IS	Independent School (Qatar)
IFC	International Finance Corporation
IMF	International Monetary Fund
ITA	Itara-e-Taleem-o-Agahi (India)
NGO	nongovernmental organization
NRSP	National Rural Support Program (Pakistan)
OECD	Organisation for Economic Co-operation and Development
PIP	Private School Implementation Partner (Pakistan)
PISA	Programme for International Student Assessment
PPP	public-private partnership
PR	Pakistan Railways
PSN	Pitagoras Network of Schools (Brazil)
SIMCE	Sistema de Medición de la Calidad de la Educación (Chile)
TIMSS	Trends in International Mathematics and Science Study
UNCTAD	United Nations Conference on Trade and Development
UNESCO	United Nations Educational, Scientific, and Cultural Organization

Introduction

Despite recent increases, enrollment rates remain low in several developing regions. Efficient and equitable access to education is proving to be elusive to many people. Often low-income families, girls, indigenous peoples, and other poor and marginalized groups have only limited access to education. Several Sub-Saharan African and South Asian countries have yet to achieve universal primary coverage, even though enrollment rates across all developing countries increased from 81 percent in 1991 to 86 percent in 2006. The quality of education, as measured by standardized tests, is low and represents a major challenge. The majority of students from those developing countries who participate in international assessments score poorly, and this is the case even in the absence of most low-income countries, which tend not to participate in such assessments.

Given market failures and equity concerns, the public sector remains an important player in providing education services, but making high-quality education accessible for all in developing countries requires innovative programs and initiatives in addition to public resources and leadership. There are ways in which the public and private sectors can join together to complement each other's strengths in providing education services and helping developing countries to meet the Millennium Development Goals for education and to improve learning outcomes. These public-private partnerships (PPPs) can even be tailored and targeted specifically to meet the needs of low-income communities.

The concept of a public-private partnership (PPP) recognizes the existence of alternative options for providing education services besides public finance and public delivery. Although there are many forms of PPPs, including partnerships where private organizations support the education sector through philanthropic activities and high-engagement ventures, this study examines PPPs in which the government guides policy and provides financing while the private sector delivers education services to students. In particular, governments contract out private providers to supply a specified service of a defined quantity and quality at an agreed price for a specific period of time. These contracts contain rewards and sanctions for nonperformance and include situations in which the private sector shares the financial risk in the delivery of public services.

This partial definition covers several types of contracts, depending on the specific services provided. The contracts vary in their degree of complexity. For education, the services provided can range from the construction, management, or maintenance of infrastructure (often referred to as a private finance initiative) to the provision of education services and operations, as in voucher schemes or charter schools.

Building on previous work, the international literature, the results of recently completed and ongoing impact evaluations, and the *World Development Report 2004* (World Bank 2003a) framework, this book presents a conceptualization of the issues related to PPPs, a detailed review of studies with rigorous evaluations, and guidelines on how to create successful PPPs in education. The World Bank has been involved in exploring the private sector's participation in the provision of public goods for several years (see Bell 1995 for a general overview).

PPPs have been studied in depth in health (World Bank 2003b; Harding 2002) and in education (Jallade 1973; Blomqvist and Jimenez 1989; Lockheed and van Eeghen 1998; James 1993; LaRocque and Patrinos 2006; World Bank 2006). Recent contributions to the literature are the proceedings from a conference jointly organized by the World Bank and Harvard University in 2005 (Chakrabarti and Peterson 2008; Patrinos and Sosale, 2007). Also, the World Bank held a follow-up international conference on PPPs in 2007 where six rigorous studies of PPPs in education were presented.

This book shows how PPPs can facilitate service delivery and lead to additional financing for the education sector as well as expand equitable access and improve learning outcomes. It goes on to discuss the best way to set up these arrangements. A wide range of education contracting models exists, and all of them have the potential to improve the education system. However, few existing programs have been evaluated, and too few of these evaluations are rigorous. Nevertheless, it is possible to glean some information about promising approaches from a careful review of the existing studies.

Private providers are playing an increasingly important role in education

Private participation in education has increased dramatically over the last two decades across the world, serving all types of communities—from high-income to low-income families. Although governments remain the main financiers of education (at least of primary and secondary education), in many countries private agents deliver a sizable share of education (table 1). A number of governments contract with the private sector to provide some of the services involved in producing education, such as teacher training, management, or curriculum design. Other governments contract with a private organization to manage and operate a public school, as is the case with charter and concession schools. Still other contracts require private organizations to provide education to a specific group of students by means of a subsidy, a contract, or a voucher. In the most common type of PPP, the government provides subsidies to existing private schools or to fund student places. The continuum of the extent to which countries are using PPPs ranges from those in which education is provided only by the public sector to those in which it is largely publicly funded and privately provided.

Some countries make a sharp distinction between the role of the public sector as education financier and that of the private sector as education provider. For instance, in the Netherlands, all education is publicly financed, including private schools, which enroll more than two-thirds of all students. In other countries, the private sector plays an important role in providing education, but the government only subsidizes some of the students who attend private schools (for example, Chile). Several African countries have different types of nonpublic schools, including government-subsidized independent schools (for example, the Gambia), partially subsidized mission or religious

Table 1 Growing private enrollment rate in education, 1990 and 2005, selected countries

Country	Primary %			Secondary %		
	1990	2005	% Change	1990	2005	% Change
Benin	3	12	300	8	25	213
Brazil	14	10	−29	35	12	−66
Bulgaria	0	0	0	0	1	100
Chile	39	51	31	49	52	6
Colombia	15	19	27	39	24	−38
India[a]	10	20	100	10	23	130
Indonesia	18	17	−6	49	44	−10
Jordan	23	30	30	6	16	167
Netherlands	69	69	0	83	83	0
Pakistan[b]	25	27	8	24	25	4
Peru	13	16	23	15	22	47
South Africa	1	2	100	2	3	50
Thailand	10	16	60	16	13	−19
Togo	25	42	68	17	28	65
Tunisia	1	1	0	12	5	−58
Ukraine	0	0	0	0	0	0
United States	10	10	0	10	9	−10

Sources: Kingdon 2007; www.uis.unesco.org; www.worldbank.org/education/edstats; www.oecd.org.
Note: Compatibility across countries is limited because of different definitions of education expenditure. However, compatibility within each country across years is ensured. Most recent data available within two years of the year indicated.
a. Rural, based on household surveys.
b. Based on household surveys.

schools (for example, Lesotho), and at least partially subsidized community-organized schools (for example, Kenya). Elsewhere, some countries have public schools that are supported financially by the private sector (for example, Pakistan). Overall, the private sector's participation at the primary school level has grown more than its participation at the secondary level, but there is significant variation across countries. While overall private participation is typically higher at the secondary level, private participation at all levels continues to grow. One way to categorize the types of PPPs is to separate financing from provision (figure 1).

Figure 1 Financing and provision of services in public-private partnerships

Finance		Provision: Private	Provision: Public
	Private	• Private schools • Private universities • Home schooling • Tutoring	• User fees • Student loans
	Public	• Vouchers • Contract schools • Charter schools • Contracting out	• Public schools • Public universities

Source: Adapted from World Bank 2006.

The governments of many developed countries have found a range of different ways to leverage the capacity and expertise of the private sector to provide education. In a subset of OECD (Organisation for Economic Co-operation and Development) countries, more than one-fifth of public expenditure is transferred to private institutions, either directly or by subsidizing households to pay for the school of their choice. Moreover, on average, OECD countries spend 12 percent of their education budgets in education institutions that are privately managed. These governments have financed a wide variety of schools on a per pupil basis to meet demand for different kinds of schooling. In the United States, the number of private companies providing supplemental academic services (academic tutoring) increased by 90 percent in just one year, between 2003 and 2004. This sharp increase was partly driven by the 45 percent increase in federal funds allocated to supplemental education between 2001 and 2005.

In several developing countries, governments subsidize private schools, mostly operated by faith-based nonprofit organizations, by financing either school inputs, such as teacher salaries and textbooks, or per pupil grants. Although schools managed by faith-based organizations and local communities are often not considered to be strictly private, in this book the term "private" encompasses the whole range of nongovernment providers of education services. Across the world, enrollment in private primary schools grew by 58 percent between 1991 and 2004, while enrollment in public primary schools grew by only 10 percent. Globally, there are approximately 113 million students in nongovernment schools; 51 million are at the secondary level.

Public-private partnerships are also being used to build school infrastructure. PPPs are a useful way to increase the funding available for constructing or upgrading school buildings and often yield better value for money than traditional public sector investments. In such partnerships, the government usually contracts a private company to build and/or maintain school buildings on a long-term basis, typically 25 to 30 years. In this type of PPP, the private sector supplier assumes responsibility for the risk inherent in the ownership and efficient operation of the project's facilities. This method of financing school buildings is used in many OECD countries but most extensively in the United Kingdom. In recent years, several developing countries have also tried this approach, though it is too early to see results.

Private education providers are also playing an increasingly important role in delivering education to low-income families. They include a range of school operators including faith-based organizations, local communities, nongovernmental organizations (NGOs), and private for-profit and not-for-profit schools. Some African and South Asian countries, where demand exceeds the supply of school places and public funds are limited, have experienced growth in the number of private low-cost schools that cater to low-income students, mostly at the secondary level.

The arguments in favor of public-private partnerships

The theoretical literature on the topic suggests four positive outcomes of the private provision of public services:

- *PPPs can create competition in the education market.* The private sector can compete for students with the public sector. In turn, the public sector has an incentive to react to this competition by increasing the quality of the education that it provides.
- *PPP contracts can be more flexible than most public sector arrangements.* Generally, the public sector has less autonomy in hiring teachers and organizing schools than the private sector does. Public-private contracts can be a better fit between the supply of and demand for education. Flexibility in teacher contracting is one of the primary motivations for PPPs.
- *Governments can choose private providers in PPP contracts by means of an open bidding process in which the government defines specific requirements for the quality of education that it demands from the contractor.* The contracts often include measurable outcomes and clauses that specify the condition to deliver a certain quality of education, and the contractor with the best or lowest cost proposal is then chosen. This one characteristic of the contract alone can raise the quality of education.
- *PPP contracts can achieve an increased level of risk-sharing between the government and the private sector.* This risk-sharing is likely to increase efficiency in the delivery of services and, consequently, to induce the channeling of additional resources to the provision for education.

So increasing the private sector's role in education can have several potential advantages over the traditional public delivery of education. Whether these benefits are actually realized depends greatly on how well designed the partnership between the public and private sector is, on the regulatory framework of the country, and on the capacity of the government to oversee and enforce its contracts and partnerships with the private sector. When a PPP is implemented correctly, it can increase efficiency and choice and expand access to education services, particularly for households that tend to be poorly served by traditional delivery methods. PPPs also allow governments to take advantage of the specialized skills offered by certain private organizations and to overcome operating restrictions such as inflexible salary scales and work rules that may prevail in the public sector.

Another advantage is that governments can contract out to the private sector in a range of initiatives that can include everything from nonacademic activities such as food services and management contracts involving a few schools, to subsidizing the tuition at private schools for hundreds of thousands of students, to long-term, multimillion dollar infrastructure partnerships. For policymakers, contracting is a middle ground between government delivery and outright privatization and does not attract as much controversy and criticisms as privatization. Contracting can also enable governments to target initiatives towards particular groups in society or to achieve specific outcomes. In addition, it is a way to bring the private sector's skills and resources into the education sector (as is the case of capital investments for school construction under private finance initiatives) and to increase efficiency and innovation in the delivery of education. Contracting can do all of this while allowing governments to keep schools accountable.

The arguments against public-private partnerships

There is a body of literature that argues that there are negative outcomes associated with the private provision of public services:

- PPPs will lead to the privatization of education and thus will reduce the government's control over a public service.
- Increasing the educational choices available to students and their families may increase socioeconomic segregation if better prepared students end up self-selecting into high-quality schools, thus further improving their outcomes.
- PPPs will lead to poorer students being left behind in the deteriorating public schools that lose the support of more educated parents.

PPPs may face resistance from certain stakeholders. For instance, teachers and other employees may see PPPs as a threat to their job stability, while teachers' and public sector unions may see them as a way of diminishing their influence over their members' terms and conditions of service. Policymakers need to take these points of view into account when designing their contracting initiatives. They should consult with stakeholders and share the contract documentation with them. It may also be useful for policymakers to recruit leading figures in the politics and business communities who understand the potential benefits of PPPs and can use their influence to help to overcome any resistance.

There can also be some challenges and risks involved in PPPs. Inputs to education, processes, and outputs are very different and require several different forms of contracts (including management, support, professional, operational, educational services, and infrastructure). All of these variations need to be assessed separately as they require different approaches in order to be effective. For example, in many countries, it is likely that the capacity of public agencies will have to be developed before it will be possible to expand the schooling options available to low-income students. In some cases, there may even be a need to build the capacity of private operators to deliver high-quality schooling.

While one advantage of PPPs is that they can be a more cost-effective way to provide education than the tradition public sector approach, there are some instances in which this may not be the case. For example, contracting for facility availability may be more expensive than traditional procurement methods when the costs of awarding and managing contracts or of private borrowing are particularly high. Also, if poorly handled, contracting can even reduce already low levels of government accountability and control (Kingdon 2007). It can also create opportunities for corruption in the awarding of the contracts. Therefore, partnerships that provide financing to private schools but do not demand accountability can have negative consequences (Kingdon 2007).

In countries where PPPs have not been extensively tried before, the government may need to change its education policies and regulatory framework. The government must clearly create an enabling framework that includes:

- defining the place of private providers in the national education strategy;
- setting clear, objective, and streamlined criteria that the private sector must meet in order to establish and operate schools;
- introducing school funding systems that integrate public and private schools and that are neutral, responsive, and targeted;
- establishing an effective quality assurance system.

Good design cannot ensure the success of a PPP in education as it must also be implemented effectively and efficiently. To ensure this, governments should choose their private partners by means of a transparent, competitive, and multi-stage selection process. Second, they should assign the roles of purchaser and provider of education services to different entities within the education administrative agencies. Third, they must ascertain that the private agency in question has sufficient capacity for the task at hand. Also, government education institutions must develop their own capacity, establish quality assurance mechanisms, develop appropriate performance measures for contractors, and devise incentives to achieve performance targets as well as sanctions for nonperformance.

The evidence

The existing evidence from around the world shows that the correlation between private provision of education and indicators of education quality is positive, which suggests that the private sector can deliver high-quality education at a low cost. Using data from the OECD's Programme for International Student Assessment, Woessmann (2005) showed that publicly operated schools deliver lower test scores than privately operated schools, but publicly funded private schools are associated with higher academic achievement than publicly operated institutions. Therefore, partnerships in which the private sector is the operator and the public sector is the financier have the potential to increase enrollment while keeping the education budget in check.

Also, although more rigorous evidence is needed, it is clear that PPPs, contracting, and subsidy arrangements can rapidly expand access to schooling and increase its quality, especially if coupled with rigorous quality assurance mechanisms and such interventions as teacher training and school improvement initiatives. In doing so, it particularly benefits marginalized groups and the poor who are ill served by traditionally delivered public services. Private school contracting programs and programs involving the private management of public schools can provide the poor with low-cost or free access to education. In fact, these contracting initiatives are usually aimed directly at the poor, including the schools run by Fe y Alegría, a Jesuit order that provides education in remote rural areas, under contract to the governments of several Latin American countries.

Strategic use of the private sector has led to the rapid expansion of access to education in several countries. Senegal and Tanzania deregulated the secondary education sector at a relatively low cost and a positive correlation with enrollment. Colombia's targeted voucher program provided places in private secondary schools for more than 100,000 students from poor families. Several rigorous evaluations have shown the program to be a success (Angrist et al. 2002; Angrist, Bettinger, and Kremer 2006). Voucher students were more likely to pass college entrance exams, had higher graduation rates, and scored better on standardized tests. The program cost less than public secondary schools on a per pupil basis. In Bangladesh, BRAC's (Bangladesh Rural Advancement Committee) Non-Formal Primary Education Program started in 1985 with 22 one-room schools. By 2007, it was serving more than 1.5 million children in more than 20,000 pre-primary and 32,000 primary schools, which accounted for 11 percent of primary school children in

Bangladesh. BRAC schools teach the same competencies as government schools, but they enroll and retain a higher proportion of hard-to-reach children, such as girls, who constitute 65 percent of students. There was a boom in the creation of private schools in Pakistan between 2000 and 2005, with 15,000 new private schools being set up. This increase happened to an equal extent in both urban and rural areas and reached both low- and high-income households (Andrabi et al. 2008). The enrollment rate in private schools of children from the poorest households in rural areas jumped from 0 percent to 6 percent. The private schools charge very low fees, less than 10 cents a day (Andrabi et al. 2006). In this way, private provision has increased enrollment in rural areas and among low-income households at a very low cost. These examples show that, when implemented correctly, PPPs can help countries to satisfy unmet demand for schooling.

With regard to the effects of charter schools, some useful lessons have emerged from a small set of empirical studies. Based on evidence from Colombia and Venezuela, it is known that the private management of public schools has a positive impact on student test scores. However, we know less about precisely which characteristics of charter and concession schools (publicly funded, privately operated schools) make them perform better than public schools, other than perhaps fewer civil service constraints, more school autonomy, and the increased length of the school year. Nonetheless, it seems from existing evaluations that flexibility in the contract is an important factor in determining positive education outcomes.

As for vouchers, they are associated with much controversy. In several countries, governments allow parents to send their children to the school of their choice, fund private and religious schools from the public budget, and allocate resources to schools based on enrollment. These types of programs deliver similar benefits to those offered in voucher programs. Some of these arrangements are over 100 years old (such as those in Denmark and the Netherlands) while others are more recent (such as those in Chile and Sweden). Colombia's targeted voucher program has been subject to extensive analysis because of its randomized design. These evaluations have shown that the program is well targeted, effective, and efficient. The evidence from Chile's voucher program is mixed and controversial. Some studies have found that it has had several positive outcomes, but other studies have challenged this, arguing that the original studies had problems of selection and a lack of adequate instruments. Furthermore, for many years following the voucher reform of 1981, overall education quality in Chile did not improve (Hsieh and Urquiola 2006). More recently, there have been some rapid increases in test scores and an ongoing revision of the school financing formula as an attempt to reduce equity concerns. Universal school choice (where all parents in a country can choose their children's schools by means of a voucher) in Europe has led to a more competitive schools market. In most cases, this competition yields better outcomes overall, as would be predicted by theory. Nevertheless, there is much that we still need to learn about school choice and vouchers.

Some of the evidence of the impact of public provision of private services on education outcomes, including measures of student achievement, is positive but is not enough to justify either ignoring PPPs or expanding them on a large scale. The few studies that have been carried out so far suggest that contracting out to the private sector can have several benefits, including greater efficiency, increased choice, and wider access to education, particularly for those households who have been poorly served by traditional methods of providing education. In general, private management of public schools tends to be efficient and yield higher test scores than public institutions when students reach the end of basic education. In addition, despite being controversial, vouchers can improve academic outcomes, especially for the poor.

However, few of the existing empirical studies of PPPs can be considered to have yielded robust conclusions. There is a need to evaluate how PPPs work most effectively in different contexts, particularly where contracting models need to be improved or fine-tuned and in countries where partnerships are still nascent. While much is known about funding school choice, much less is known about which characteristics of charter and concession schools make them perform better than public schools. More research is also needed on universal versus targeted school choice and on private finance initiatives. These programs should be piloted and rigorously evaluated in different settings. Because of the pressing need to increase the evidence base in these areas, this study provides guidance on how to carry out better evaluations of a variety of aspects of public-private partnerships in education.

Spotlight on the Netherlands

The Netherlands provides a model of school choice that delivers access and quality education; an example of the potential of public-private partnerships in education.

One of the key features of the Dutch education system is freedom of education—freedom to establish schools, determine the principles on which the school is based, and organize classroom teaching. In fact, the Netherlands has one of the oldest national systems based on school choice in the world. Although all schools in the Netherlands are government funded, most are administered by private school boards. As a result, most children in the Netherlands attend private schools, a trend that has been increasing over the past 150 years. Parents can choose among several schools, and school choice is often promoted by the government as a way to increase competition in the school system. Efficiency increases as public and private schools try to improve their outcomes to develop a good reputation and thus attract more students.

In the Dutch education system, education policy is determined centrally but the administration and management of schools is decentralized at the school level. The central government exercises ultimate control over both public and private schools. Students from the Netherlands do exceptionally well on international academic achievement tests such as the Third International Mathematics and Science Study (TIMMS). The Netherlands scored near the top in reading and math in 2003 and was the top performer in mathematics and science achievement for the final years of secondary school in 1995. The country achieves high scores even after controlling for national income and expenditure per student. Thus, the system is not only successful academically but is also cost effective, yielding good results at relatively low cost. Previous research has found that religious schools perform slightly better than public schools in academic achievement. More recent research has shown that the substantial degree of competition in the system is one determinant of its high academic achievement rates. Thus, a large school choice system can promote efficiency and equity without necessarily leading to privatization or reduced public scrutiny. All this lends

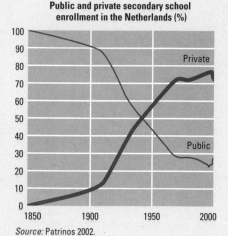

Public and private secondary school enrollment in the Netherlands (%)

Source: Patrinos 2002.

credence to the arguments of the proponents of school choice. However, the question remains whether these outcomes can be expected in other countries or whether the Netherlands is unique. If they can be generalized, what can other countries do to promote academic achievement and to ensure they are accessing all available resources, both private and public?

Sources: Netherlands Ministry of Education 2002; James 1984; Justesen 2002.

Understanding Public-Private Partnerships in Education

The main rationale for developing public-private partnerships (PPPs) in education is to maximize the potential for expanding equitable access to schooling and for improving education outcomes, especially for marginalized groups. In this chapter, we show how different types of contracts can help meet these two objectives in different socioeconomic and political contexts. Specifically, we examine how contracts are used to hold all partners accountable and how contracts are designed to produce measurable improvements in education outcomes or performance. The analysis considers contracting as a distinct instrument from any other education accountability mechanisms. We define *contracting* as the process whereby a government procures education or education-related services of a defined quantity and quality at an agreed price from a specific provider. The agreement between the funder and the service provider is recorded in a contract and is valid for a specified period of time (Taylor 2003; Wang 2000).

The *World Development Report 2004* (World Bank 2003a) concluded that services can be provided to poor people most successfully when citizens, service providers, and governments are accountable to each other. Contracts can improve service delivery by clearly assigning responsibilities among these actors, identifying objectives and outputs, gathering information on the performance and progress of the contractor, and ensuring the enforceability of the provisions of the contract.

Many forms of contracting are currently used in education around the world. A range of different services can be procured from the private sector (table 1.1). Some

governments buy the services involved in producing education (inputs), such as teacher training, management, curriculum design, or the use of a school facility from private organizations (Savas 2000). Other governments contract with private organizations to provide the process of education, for example, by managing and operating public schools. Some other governments contract with private organizations to provide education to specific students (thus, buying outputs). The challenges and potential benefits of contracting for services that are inputs, processes, or outputs are very different and are thus discussed separately.

This chapter discusses each type of education service: (i) management services, (ii) professional services, (iii) support services, (iv) operational services, (v) education services, (vi) facility availability, and (vii) facility availability and education services combined.

chapter 1

Table 1.1 Types of contracts in education

What governments contract for	What governments buy
Management, professional, support services (input)	• School management (financial and human resources management)
	• Support services (meals and transportation)
	• Professional services (teacher training, curriculum design, textbook delivery, quality assurance, and supplemental services)
Operational services (process)	• The education of students, financial and human resources management, professional services, and building maintenance
Education services (outputs)	• Student places in private schools (by contracting with schools to enroll specific students)
Facility availability (inputs)	• Infrastructure and building maintenance
Facility availability and education services (both inputs and outputs)	• Infrastructure combined with services (operational or educational outputs)

Source: Adapted from World Bank 2006.

Management services

Weak management is an important constraint to improving public school performance. To deal with this problem, some governments have brought in private organizations to manage either a single public school or an entire public school district. The responsibilities that the contractor assumes under these contracts usually fall into four categories: financial management, staff management, long-term planning, and leadership. Within these contracts, all nonmanagerial personnel continue to be public sector employees. Management contracts have several potential benefits for public education, including bringing in professional skills and new ideas from the private sector, giving managers the freedom to manage, reducing the bureaucratic and union constraints associated with public service employment, promoting competition among organizations bidding to win the management contract, and enabling education authorities to specify performance requirements so that they can change contractors if performance is unsatisfactory.

PPPs in the area of management services can work, but these services are inherently more difficult to contract out than some other services. Specifying and monitoring the performance of managers, as distinct from the organization overall, is difficult. Because many factors contribute to school performance besides the quality of management, it would be inappropriate to attribute changes in school performance simply to the effects of the management contract. In most countries, the gains from contracting out input services have built up over time as the governments gradually become better at creating these kinds of contracts.

Professional services

Contracting out professional services such as teacher training, textbook delivery, curriculum design, quality certification, and supplemental services is straightforward and usually successful. Its main advantage is that it brings private providers' expertise to bear on improving public education. The content and oversight of contracts are both critical when buying input services. Simple input services are relatively easy to specify in contractual terms, and the performance of contractors can also be conveniently monitored. In other words, the quality of service can be specified in the contract and sanctions included if the contractor fails to provide that level of quality. In addition, competitive pressures can give providers an incentive to maximize their performance because contract cancellation is a credible threat as there are plenty of providers of input services in most countries. Because an organization can be contracted to deliver input services to many different schools, economies of scale can be achieved. The benefits that come from specialization—reduced costs and better quality—can also be easily achieved.

If public sector staff originally provided the services, then the handover to the contractors can be difficult. The early phases of contracting can be daunting for officials who may be unfamiliar with the process and who may lack the know-how to establish contracts. However, while it can be challenging to gain political acceptance for contracting out support and professional services, this move usually yields demonstrably positive results, including cost savings, quality improvements, and more time for school officials to devote to education (World Bank 2006).

Support services

Noninstructional activities, including building maintenance, pupil transportation, and school meals, are often very costly for public schools. In the few cases where good cost analyses have been done, these services have often been found to cost significantly more in public schools than in private schools (World Bank 2006). The proportion of nonteaching school staff is often high in public schools, and salary studies in several countries have found that the wages of support staff are higher in public schools than for similar jobs in the private sector. In response, policymakers in many countries have expanded the extent to which they contract out support services to increase cost-effectiveness and free up the time and resources of school staff and education officials so that they can focus on the learning process. Usually, one contract is tendered to cover multiple schools so that the contracts are large enough to attract many bidders.

Contracting out support services enables the education sector to take advantage of the expertise and the efficient organization of private companies with expertise in specific activities, and of the economies of scale that result when the same contractor provides services for many schools. It also allows school staff to concentrate on teaching. Also, in those countries where public sector staff is paid high wages as a result of belonging to strong unions, there is a cost saving associated with the contractor being able to hire nonunionized labor (World Bank 2006). Some contracting out of support services is done in virtually every public education system in the world. For example, public school authorities hardly ever run food services in schools in developed countries.

Operational services

In some countries, the education authorities contract private organizations to handle a wider range of responsibilities, in essence, to operate an entire public school. In these operational contracts, private organizations not only manage the school but staff it as well (World Bank 2006). The aim of such contracts is most often to free schools from public service constraints or to give schools more autonomy and to improve the oversight of the school by tapping into the interest and knowledge of parents and other community members. In many cases where schools are allowed to govern themselves, communities also contribute to the construction, upkeep, or improvement of facilities (either in-kind or financially). Sometimes education authorities initiate a contracting arrangement in response to demand from a community organization or a nonprofit education organization (World Bank 2003a).

Operational services contracting is usually tried in problem areas, making it a viable mechanism for improving schools with performance problems and for ensuring service delivery to "hard-to-reach"

populations (World Bank 2006). Also, this type of contract can be targeted to disadvantaged populations (Barrera-Osorio 2007).

Education services

Instead of engaging a private organization to operate a public school, some governments contract out the enrollment of students in private schools, thus, in essence, buying outputs. By paying for students to enroll in existing schools, governments can quickly expand access without incurring any up-front expenditure on constructing and equipping new schools. Other governments contract out students' enrollment in specialized services that are not available in the public sector. Thus, the concept of contracting out education services involves using public funds to underwrite individual student enrollment in existing schools. This type of contract can be targeted to specific students and groups, such as low-income, disadvantaged, or "problem" students.

Contracting for education services also makes it possible to leverage private schools' investments in their school capital assets by sending publicly funded students to these schools. As a result, the publicly funded students receive a higher quality education than if the cost of their education had been restricted simply to the amount of public funding spent on them. Also, if the contracted schools are willing to subsidize publicly funded students from the fees paid by their paying students (as many nonprofit schools do), this form of contracting allows publicly funded students to benefit from the higher fees paid by privately funded students (World Bank 2006).

This type of contract enhances accountability in two ways. First, schools are subject to competitive pressures because parents and students are able to choose from among public and private schools. Second, in some cases school operators are selected through competitive processes that give schools an incentive to improve their services. Moreover, accountability is assured by pre-existing school governance and oversight arrangements, such as school boards, boards of trustees, and parent committees (World Bank 2006).

Facility availability

In many countries, governments have managed to mobilize private investment to finance needed capital stock in utilities and other public services. Contracting out the provision of facilities is appealing because it relieves governments of having to finance capital investments up-front and all at once. In the education and health sectors, the government is often the major or only purchaser of services for the new facility, which puts an important burden on the public purse all at once. In these cases, contracting out the financing and construction of facilities to the private sector allows the government to pay for these capital investments over time by making periodic payments over the term of the contract.

The value of the capital investment is determined completely by the government's payments. This reliance on a single customer, subject to changing political and policy priorities, makes investing in social service facilities extremely risky for private investors (World Bank 2006). As a result, contracting private institutions to finance and build schools is much more challenging than other types of contracting. Therefore, much of the process and content of the contract involves minimizing the risk of the government defaulting and making the investment safer and, hence, more appealing to private investors.

The scope of the responsibilities taken on by the private sector varies by contract, and similar arrangements often have different names. For example, build-operate-transfer arrangements are often referred to as design-build-finance-operate (table 1.2). Under build-operate-transfer, which is the most common type of arrangement, the private sector finances, designs, constructs, and operates a public school facility under a contract with the government for a given period of time (for example, 25 to 30 years). At the end of the contract period, the ownership of the school facility is transferred to the government.

Although arrangements can differ widely, infrastructure-focused PPPs share several characteristics:

- The private consortium is selected through a competitive tender process.

- Private sector partners invest in school infrastructure and provide related services (for example, building maintenance).

- The government retains the responsibility for delivering core services such as teaching.

- Arrangements between the government and the private partner are governed by long-term contracts (usually 25 to 30 years) that specify the services the private contractor must deliver and the standards that it must meet.

- In service contracts, the private organization often takes on several functions such as design, building, maintenance, and employment of some nonteaching staff.

- Payments under the contract are contingent on the private operator successfully delivering services of an agreed performance standard.

Contracting out facility availability can have several benefits. Facilities can be built more quickly than under traditional procurement arrangements, provided that authorities have made a detailed quantification of capital costs involved and have

Table 1.2   The range of options for public-private partnerships in infrastructure

Type of partnership	Features
Traditional design and build	The government contracts with a private partner to design and build a facility to specific requirements.
Operations and maintenance	The government contracts with a private partner to operate a publicly owned facility.
Turnkey operation	The government provides financing, the private partner designs, constructs, and operates facility for a specified time period, while the public partner retains ownership of facility.
Lease-purchase	The private partner leases a facility to the government for a specified time period, after which ownership is vested with government.
Lease or own-develop-operate	The private partner leases or buys a facility from the government and develops and operates the facility under contract to the government for a specified time period.
Build-operate-transfer	The private partner obtains an exclusive contract to finance, build, operate, maintain, manage, and collect user fees for a facility for a fixed period to amortize its investment, and at the end of the franchise, the title reverts to the government.
Build-own-operate	The government either transfers ownership and responsibility for an existing facility or contracts with a private partner to build, own, and operate new facility in perpetuity.

Source: World Bank 2006.

reasonably good capital planning processes in place. Using these contracts in public education often has positive effects throughout the sector, not just in the facilities involved. For example, private involvement in the financing and construction of education facilities often results in better-maintained buildings that do not require costly renovations.

However, the long-term purchasing commitments required for contracting out the financing and construction of an education facility are difficult for many governments to manage, and the associated repayment risks can make loans obtained by the private consortiums very costly. Many governments find it difficult to set and maintain service prices high enough to allow consortiums to pay back (equity or debt) capital payments. This difficulty is compounded if the education authorities have either hidden or poorly quantified the capital costs of these public facilities at the outset, which can lead to exorbitant payments for privately provided infrastructure.

There are often only limited efficiency gains and cost savings from contracting out facility availability because of the high cost of borrowing for social infrastructure and the limited range of savings associated with the private design, construction, and operation of facilities compared with traditional public procurement. For most social services, more significant cost savings can be gained from contracting out operational services to the private sector. Capital costs, including maintenance, rarely exceed 15 percent of total service costs in education and health (World Bank 2006). Thus, nonprofit organizations are often unable to participate in contracts for the finance and construction of facilities because they have less access than for-profit organizations to the large amount of long-term finance that is needed (box 1.1).

Both facility availability and education services (comprehensive contracting)

Another form of contracting that some governments have used in the social sectors, particularly health care, but not yet

> **BOX 1.1** *Sources of capital for the nonprofit provision of education*
>
> There are only few sources of capital funding for the nonprofit provision of social services. These include:
>
> - Publicly guaranteed or subsidized bonds
> - Public subsidies
> - Private finance with a government guarantee (or quasi-guarantee)
> - Retained earnings
> - Donations
> - Long-term loans (restricted to large, corporate, nonprofit organizations)
>
> Because the first three require public sector support, they defeat the purpose of mobilizing nongovernmental finance. The last three are used to only a limited extent in most countries.
>
> *Source*: World Bank 2006.

in education, is to contract private firms to both provide and operate facilities, in other words, to undertake all of the activities associated with delivering the needed services and infrastructure. In essence, the government simultaneously implements two forms of contract with the same operator—a contract for facility financing, development, and availability and a long-term contract for providing services. The rationale cited most often for this form of contracting is that it enables governments to obtain needed capital investment while providing the operator with a considerable incentive to organize and deliver services as efficiently as possible. The efficiency gains that the private consortium can capture from both constructing and operating the schools may make up for the fact that they face higher costs of borrowing than the government.

Managing these facility availability and operations contracts is clearly challenging. It is "best practice" for private participation initiatives to be managed by the central government, often in a PPP unit attached to the finance ministry or treasury (World Bank 2006). This is done to ensure that the government rapidly develops the expertise that it needs to manage the "transaction" or capital part of the initiative. However, in the social sectors, the service purchasing contract is an integral part of the feasibility and attractiveness of the proposed private involvement. Officials from both the central unit and the sectoral ministry must work together effectively to design the two contracts (World Bank 2006). Nonetheless, their very different priorities, training, and perspectives often make it difficult for the staff of these two entities to collaborate. The contracting process itself can be expensive, which may dampen interest among potential private operators and investors because unsuccessful bidders have to absorb the considerable cost of bidding. Despite these challenges, comprehensive contracting combines the advantages of contracting out both facility availability and services, and savings and efficiencies could result from having the same organization design and build a facility in which it will deliver high-quality services at the lowest possible cost.

International Experience

While governments remain the main financiers of primary and secondary education, a substantial share of education worldwide is now delivered by private agents (Lewin and Sayed 2005). Private enrollment has increased faster than public enrollment in recent years. Enrollment in private primary education grew by 58 percent between 1991 and 2004 from 39 to 62 million, while public enrollment grew by only 10 percent from 484 to 530 million during the same period (UNESCO 2007). Sub-Saharan Africa, the Middle East, and South Asia are the regions with the largest growth in the private provision of education (UNESCO 2007).

To increase access and improve quality in education, many governments are finding it effective to separate the financing of education from its provision (World Bank 2003a). Empirical evidence suggests that education systems in which schools are publicly funded but privately operated are associated with better student performance (Schütz, West, and Woessmann 2007). So governments are exploring ways to involve the private sector in providing education. This chapter presents a global review of public-private partnerships (PPPs) in primary and secondary education, focusing on partnerships in which governments use contracts as instruments of accountability. The underlying idea behind contracts is that they introduce a performance-based approach to education because they clearly link funding and provision with education outputs and they direct services to underserved student populations, especially marginalized groups such as low-income or disadvantaged students.

In the most common type of PPP, governments fund existing private schools, mainly to increase access to education but also to enhance quality by enabling poor students to attend better private schools and by introducing school competition to promote efficiency. In more recent types of PPPs, governments have contracted with private providers to deliver a range of inputs and services with the expectation that they will introduce new pedagogical skills and management efficiencies that the public sector lacks, thus generating alternatives to traditional forms of public education. As discussed in the previous chapter, contracts for education-related services can cover a range of services and inputs including the private management of public schools, subsidies and vouchers, private finance initiatives for school construction and maintenance, and professional services such as teacher training, curriculum design, and textbook provision. The expansion of private participation in the education systems of both developed and developing countries is increasingly turning them into markets with the potential to develop innovative education methods.

In the following chapters, we discuss examples of public-private partnerships from around the world. These countries and programs are described in more detail in appendix A, which contains information on 92 PPP programs and policies across 47 countries. The PPPs are organized by contract type, as defined in chapter 1, and are listed alphabetically by country within each of these categories. The list is not exhaustive but gives a representative picture of the variety and geographical location of PPPs worldwide.

Background and trends

The private sector can play a different role depending on the socioeconomic and political scenario. Countries such as Denmark and the Netherlands have used the private sector to provide basic education for more than 100 years by financing a wide variety of schools on a per pupil basis to meet the demand for a wide variety of different kinds of schooling. More recently, in some African and Asian countries, there has been a growth of low-cost private schools aimed at students who cannot pay the high tuition charged by elite schools or who fail to meet the eligibility requirements of high-quality public or government-funded private schools (Lewin and Sayed 2005; Andrabi et al. 2007). In the former example, the private sector was introduced to the education sector by policy design whereas in the latter it emerged by default in order to fulfill a need.

The rise of the private sector's involvement in the education sector reflects a broader shift of public service responsibilities to the private sector. For instance, between 2003 and 2004, the number of approved private providers of supplemental services in basic and secondary education in the United States increased by 90 percent, from 997 to 1,890, while the amount of federal funds available for private contracting increased by 45 percent between 2001 and 2005 (Burch, Steinberg, and Donovan 2007). In response, governments are developing institutions, funding mechanisms, and regulatory frameworks to take advantage of the growing capacity and expertise of the private sector to enhance public education. For example, contracts to attract private funding to build and maintain school infrastructure are spreading in European countries. Also, the governments of Colombia, Qatar, and the United States have contracted with private partners to manage public schools to cater to the differentiated demand for education, in some cases using a franchising model to take advantage of good practices and economies of scale. In several countries in the OECD (the Organization for Economic Co-operation and Development), including Denmark, New Zealand, Norway, and the United Kingdom, more than 20 percent of public expenditure is transferred to private organizations—either directly or through households—to pay for education services and maximize school choice (OECD 2007b).

The public-private partnership continuum

The PPP continuum depicts the main forms of publicly funded and privately provided education across the world. It ranges from systems where all provision is strictly public to systems where it is largely publicly funded and privately provided. This conceptual framework helps to identify the extent of a country's engagement in PPPs in education (figure 2.1). The continuum assumes that the responsibility for funding largely remains with the public sector.

Figure 2.1   The public-private partnership continuum

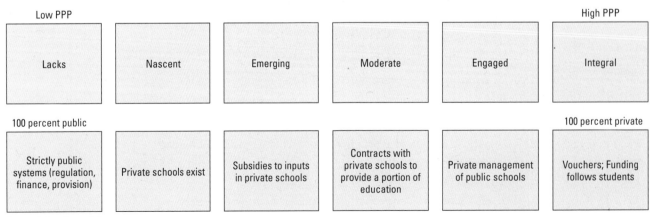

Source: Authors' compilation.

Countries in which the government is fully responsible for education and related services and assumes all regulatory and financing functions have no PPP environment. Countries that allow private schools to operate within a centrally determined regulatory framework but provide them with no funding from the public budget can be described as having a "nascent" PPP environment. In countries with a nascent PPP environment, public and private schools are independently responsible for hiring their own teachers, providing education and related services, and building school infrastructure. Students can choose between public and private schools and, in some cases, among public schools. However, they may be constrained by their families' ability to pay, academic requirements for entry, and geographical barriers to access. Mexico is an example of a country with a nascent PPP environment where 83 percent of schools at the basic level are publicly operated and no public funding is given to privately operated schools (Woessmann 2005).

Countries where the government subsidizes private schools to support their capacity to educate more students can be described as having an "emerging" PPP environment. In these countries, a lump sum from the education budget is transferred to entitled institutions based on criteria that take into account, among other factors, the socioeconomic context of the school, the number of students enrolled, and their for-profit or not-for-profit status. The subsidy is normally based on the cost of educating a student, but, because it does not necessarily follow the students' school of choice, it does not foster competition. The funds can also be applied to cover school inputs such as teachers' salaries or textbooks. The subsidy and the way it is applied in a school's budget vary by country. For example, in Argentina, 13 percent of the education budget of the local provinces is transferred to private schools with no objective criteria to guide the expenditure, and 85 percent of that money is targeted to primary schools (Villa and Duarte 2005). In Bangladesh, almost 97 percent of secondary schools are private, and most of them are heavily subsidized in the form of teacher salaries but the government's supervision of the use of resources is weak (World Bank 2003c).

A "moderate" PPP environment is evident in those countries where the government enters into contracts with private schools that require them (and pays them per pupil) to educate a specified number of students for a specified length of time, usually an academic year (World Bank 2006). As instruments of accountability, contracts establish the conditions under which the school must operate and specify the outputs that the schools are expected to produce. Contractual instruments are different from subsidy systems in that they introduce a risk-sharing element between the public and private sectors. In turn, the private sector faces the risk of financial loss for noncompliance and incentives to improve its performance (World Bank 2006). The objective of the contract is to guarantee education for low-income students when the public system lacks the capacity to do so itself (World Bank 2006).

In countries with an "engaged" PPP environment, private organizations sign an agreement with the government to manage and operate public schools in exchange for payment from the public budget. The objective of these operational contracts is to enhance the supply of education by allowing private organizations to take over failing public schools or to open new schools that take in public students. Operational contracts also aim to promote innovation on the supply side and to increase efficiency by allowing the contractors flexibility in how they manage their human and financial resources, and by relieving these schools from bureaucratic constraints (Gill et al. 2007). Communities or the contractors themselves may assume the costs of infrastructure and educational inputs, and the government then reimburses them for that expenditure. Under the Concession Schools model in Colombia, the state provides the school infrastructure and selects the students (Barrera-Osorio 2007). In contrast, in the U.S. state of Minnesota, charter schools may own school infrastructure as long as it is not purchased with state funds; they may also lease property from school boards or nonprofit organizations (Minnesota House of Representatives 2005). Private contractors usually receive payments equivalent to the per student cost of providing education (World Bank 2006). Other examples of countries with an "engaged" PPP environment include Qatar, with its independent schools, and the various Latin American countries where the Fe y Alegría network operates (Allcott and Ortega 2007; Brewer et al. 2007).

In the strongest or "integral" PPP environment, the public sector funds private schools by providing students with vouchers that will pay for their education at the school they choose to attend, thus encouraging student choice and school competition. In these countries, governments largely rely on the private sector to provide and administer education but retain regulatory and financing responsibilities. The rationale is that parents can send their children to the most productive school based on their preferences (Hanushek and Woessmann 2007). If private schools are more productive, then their enrollment will tend to increase while improvements will take place in all schools as they try to compete for potential students. Countries with an enabling environment have also devolved autonomy to schools on the grounds that keeping the locus of decision-making as close as possible to the locus of schooling produces the best learning outcomes because this makes schools accountable for their actions and outputs (World Bank 2003a). Examples include countries such as Belgium and the Netherlands, where private schools receive public funding and where 68 percent and 83 percent of secondary education enrollments are in private schools (World Bank 2008), and Chile, where one of the largest universal vouchers programs covers 38 percent of the student population (Bellei 2005).

Good outcomes can also be obtained in countries that rely on public provision. In Finland, for instance, 97 percent of enrollments are in public schools and the country is one of the top performers on the OECD's international student assessment known as Programme for International Student Assessment (PISA) (OECD 2007a). Finland has had public choice since the 1990s, and a high degree of autonomy is devolved to schools (Rinne, Kivirauma, and Simola 2002), which means that the education system is under public control but has strong autonomy and accountability features.

Public-private partnerships and the funding of existing private schools

Public-private partnerships are widespread in demand-side financing of private school operations, including vouchers, subsidies, capitation grants, and stipends; and, more recently, in contracts for the provision of education (World Bank 2006). The main objective of these PPPs is to increase access by giving families money to invest in their children's schooling by compensating them for the cost of education (Patrinos 2000). In addition, demand-side mechanisms promote parental choice, school competition, and school accountability (Gauri and Vawda 2004). Parents can choose the best schooling alternative for their children, which may induce pressure on schools to increase enrollments and to achieve better academic results at a lower cost (Hanushek and Woessmann 2007; Hoxby 2000).

Moreover, by funding parental choice, schools become accountable to families rather than to the central government, thus giving them incentives to develop innovative approaches to learning (Hanushek and Woessmann 2007). In Haiti, where socioeconomic and political problems have weakened the public sector's capacity to deliver adequate education services, 80 percent of education providers are private. One alternative way to improve access, quality, and equity outcomes is to channel public funds to nonpublic education providers within a regulatory framework that holds schools accountable for the funds that they receive and to offer support (in the form of training and technical assistance) that strengthens schools' educational and managerial capacity (box 2.1).

Critics of such policies argue that, when public funding flows to private schools, the distribution of socio-economic and educational characteristics is important in determining parental choice and that this

---

BOX 2.1 *Private schooling in Haiti*

In Haiti, 80 percent of all primary students attend nonpublic schools, which are financed by parents, religious associations, and nongovernmental organizations, among others. The quality of instruction and learning tends to be poor, and the school-based management capacity is extremely weak.

The World Bank's Haiti Education For All Adaptable Program Grant gives the management committees of eligible private schools a $90 subsidy per student so that poor students who are not enrolled in school can attend nonpublic primary schools for free. Eligibility is based on proposals submitted by the schools and are evaluated based on six criteria: (i) geographic location and related poverty classification, (ii) the quality of the education provided, (iii) governance, (iv) commitment to maximizing the enrollment capacity of the school, (v) the age of entry of students, and (vi) a demonstrated commitment to reaching children who would otherwise remain out of school. Approved proposals are sent to the Department of Administrative Affairs, which then transfers funds to the schools' bank accounts. Those private schools that receive funds are required to submit a simple financial and technical report (using a basic template) to account for their use of the funds and to indicate the numbers of students that they have enrolled.

Source: World Bank 2007b.

---

arrangement can lead to students being segregated by income level and academic achievement, with no improvement on average academic achievement (Hsieh and Urquiola 2006). Some studies suggest that in large-scale voucher programs, the positive effects of competition are limited to high-achieving students and that not all parents choose their schools based only on academic criteria (Andersen, 2008; McEwan 2001).

Universal voucher programs to increase access and introduce school choice

Several high-income countries have long had education systems that rely on voucher-like mechanisms, and most of the children in these countries who attend private schools receive vouchers. In the Netherlands, 69 percent of primary enrollment is private; in Belgium, 54 percent; and in Denmark, 12 percent (World Bank EdStats 2008). These de facto systems have been in operation for more than 100 years and fit the theoretical characteristics of more recent voucher programs designed explicitly to promote choice and competition (Andersen 2008). The most prominent features of de facto voucher systems include:

- Funding is based on expressed demand.
- All private schools share the risk that if they cannot attract enough students, they will have to close.
- Private schools have a diverse student body because they reflect the preferences of specific communities. There is an important presence of religious-oriented private schools.
- Parents are free to choose between public and private schools and, in some cases, among public schools.
- Finance and provision are separate.
- Private schools must comply with education standards defined at the central level (Andersen 2008).

There has been a move toward school-based management, in which governments devolve some or all autonomy to schools and allow them to manage and allocate their own resources to stimulate innovation (European Commission 2007). As part of decentralization reforms in the 1980s and 1990s, Chile, the Czech Republic, Hungary, and Sweden introduced system-wide vouchers that promote parental choice and enable private schools to receive public funding. In Chile, 94 percent of schools receive public funding, and over 50 percent of urban schools are private and for-profit (McEwan, Urquiola, and Vegas 2007). Private schools can choose their students and can be for-profit or not-for-profit. Almost 90 percent of subsidized schools receive co-funding from parents (Contreras, Bustos, and Sepulveda 2008). In Sweden, the reform authorized student choice and public funding for a wide variety of operators, including for-profit corporations. Unlike in Chile, Swedish public and private schools are subject to the same rules and receive the same amount per pupil, and private schools do not charge fees, making them a real option for poorer students (Ahlin 2003). In the Czech Republic and Hungary, market incentives introduced after communism led to a growth in private schooling, mostly at the secondary level (Filer and Münich 2000).

Several African countries subsidize private schools, mostly faith-based nonprofit organizations, either with school inputs (such as teacher salaries and textbooks) or through per pupil grants. The Gambia, Mauritius, and Zimbabwe rely substantially on private schools to deliver public education (LaRocque 2008). Recently, the attempt to achieve universal enrollment in basic education coupled with limited public funding has increased demand across Africa to such an extent that this has fueled a growth in the number of private low-cost schools that cater to low-income students, mostly at the secondary level (Lewin and Sayed 2005). This has given rise to a two-tier system, with a few well-funded private schools that cater to high-performing students and many private schools with no government support that do not perform as well (Verspoor 2008). Although many African countries recognize the importance of private schools in meeting demand and have found ways to expand access to education, the quality of the education and equity of access remain challenges (Verspoor 2008).

The experience in Africa demonstrates the importance of strengthening the capacity of the public agencies responsible for regulating, monitoring, and contracting private schools. It is also important to facilitate the access that private operators have to capital and technical assistance to improve their education and management practices and to create institutions to implement PPPs and guarantee flows of information to parents on school characteristics (Verspoor 2008).

Targeted voucher programs can reduce inequity

Targeted voucher programs are a useful way to widen access to higher quality schools, and to reduce inequity and constraints to access and achievement gaps for girls, disadvantaged, hard-to-reach, and minority students (Angrist et al. 2002; Carnoy and McEwan 2001). Bangladesh (1994–2001) had a program that gave stipends to girls who had demonstrated high attendance rates, scored high in school exams, and stayed unmarried until the age of 18 or until they had obtained a secondary school certificate. The program substantially increased girls' enrollment but no effort was made to increase the number of teachers to avoid overcrowded classes (Raynor and Wesson 2006). A similar program in Pakistan helped to solve the undersupply of education services in urban areas by encouraging existing private schools to open new facilities and thus create economies of scale, but the program was less successful in rural schools, which had more difficulty in hiring teachers and suffered from a higher turnover (Orazem 2000).

Colombia's secondary school voucher program, Programa de Ampliacion de Cobertura de la Educacion Secundaria, which benefited 125,000 students between 1991 and 1997 in low-income neighborhoods, yielded several good practices. The program increased secondary enrollment rates by allowing parents to choose among private schools and by providing a renewable voucher as long as the student met the academic requirements needed to move on to the following grade (Angrist et al. 2002). To ensure accurate targeting, the program required students to prove that they lived in a low-income neighborhood and that they had already been admitted into a participating private school. An alternative method of targeting is to use funding formulas that favor students from lower-income families. For instance, in South Africa, public and private schools are categorized by their poverty level and receive subsidies depending on the level of tuition fees that they charge their students (Lewin and Sayed 2005), with the poorest schools receiving the highest subsidies.

Education service contracts include quality output specifications

When governments contract out education services, they contract with existing private schools to educate a specific number of students in exchange for a per pupil payment. The contract introduces accountability and risk-sharing between governments and private providers in the provision of education. More countries have subsidized private schools or adopted voucher programs than have experimented with contracting out education services.

Contracting out basic education services is part of Colombia's strategy to increase coverage of vulnerable populations (World Bank 2006). Local governments are responsible for managing and supervising these contracts within parameters established at the national level. The local governments carry out a tendering process and encourage competition by requesting proposals from private operators. They then assign beneficiary students to selected schools except in Cali, where families are allowed to select the private school of their choice, which encourages schools to compete to attract students (World Bank 2006).

The government of Côte d'Ivoire pays private secondary schools a fixed amount to educate a student under a contracting scheme. The private schools must be certified and meet several criteria to receive subsidies, including meeting input specifications and quality indicators and having prior experience in the education market (Sakellariou and Patrinos 2008). Uganda's universal secondary education policy was introduced in 2007 to boost enrollment at the secondary level by contracting out the education of students that are not served by public and government-aided schools in exchange for fixed a per student fee. Each party's responsibilities are specified in a memorandum of understanding that requires private schools to provide authorities with performance data on a range of agreed indicators, to submit progress reports, and to be subject to periodic reviews and assessments of academic performance (LaRocque 2008). In the province of Punjab, Pakistan, the Foundation Assisted Schools Program introduced vouchers to increase enrollment and improve quality in poor areas using accountability mechanisms that link increases in access with quality measures (box 2.2).

BOX 2.2 *Punjab Education Foundation: Foundation Assisted Schools, Pakistan*

The Punjab Education Foundation was established in 1991 and restructured in 2004 into an autonomous and independent institution to promote high-quality education for the poor through partnerships with the private sector. It is funded by the government of the Punjab province of Pakistan and is headed by a 15-member, government-appointed board of directors, the majority of whom are from the private sector.

The Foundation Assisted Schools Program aims to improve education quality by taking full advantage of the capacity of the mushrooming number of private schools in Punjab. Approximately 33 percent of children aged 6 to 10 who attend school are enrolled in private schools, and private enrollment shares are on the rise. The program attempts to improve quality through three fundamental components: vouchers, teacher training, and monetary incentives to schools for improved academic performance.

The accountability components include:

Requirements for Eligibility. At least two-thirds of students have to score at least 33 percent in an academic test as a prerequisite to receive vouchers. In addition, schools have to meet other basic school input requirements, largely of a nonquantifiable nature, that are evaluated by inspectors.

A Specialized Institution to Manage PPPs. The program is managed by an independent institution, the Punjab Education Foundation, which is fully funded by the provincial government and whose mandate is to use public-private mechanisms to increase access to and improve the quality of the province's low-cost private education sector. Advantages of having a special institution include less bureaucratic pressure on schools from traditional government institutions and the potential to introduce special management practices in contracting.

Incentives and Sanctions Related to Performance. The program includes performance-based incentives at the school and teacher levels. Monetary awards are granted to the school that demonstrates the highest pass rate, and actual test scores are taken into account. Teachers in schools with high pass rates are entitled to direct monetary bonuses. If schools fail to meet minimum academic, infrastructure, or teaching requirements for three consecutive years, they are banned from the program.

Sources: World Bank staff; Punjab Education Foundation Web site (www.pef.edu.pk).

Public-private partnerships that bring alternative operators into the education system

Involving private organizations in activities beyond providing education services has expanded the education market and produced new forms of public-private engagement. Outsourcing education-related services is justified because private expertise and education innovations can add value to public education, but there are two more advantages to contracting external providers to support different aspects of the operation of public schools. First, competition between multiple providers can improve the quality of the services that they provide and can reduce costs. Second, economies of scale can result when contractors service multiple schools (World Bank 2006).

Professional and support services

Governments can hire private organizations to provide a range of support services to public and private schools that cater to low-income students. In many countries, the capacity of the public sector to deliver high-quality education is compromised by a lack of knowledge of effective pedagogical practices. To mitigate this, governments can contract with private organizations that have had proven successes with their education methods to provide certain key services such as teacher training, curriculum design, textbook provision, and supplemental services for public or private schools educating poor students.

For example, in Colombia, public authorities contract with the Escuela Nueva Foundation to train rural school teachers, distribute textbooks, and update curricula. The Foundation also provides technical assistance to rural schools to help them to implement the Escuela Nueva model, which is a multi-grade school model that has improved core education practices in Colombia's rural areas (Benveniste and McEwan 2000). The objective of the Escuela Nueva Foundation is to assure quality control and promote the sustainability of the Escuela Nueva model as it expands nationally and internationally.

The Ministries of Education in the Dominican Republic and El Salvador have also contracted out services to the Escuela Nueva Foundation to support and strengthen the program's implementation. The Escuela Nueva Foundation usually assumes part of the total value of the contract by donating textbooks or by making some other in-kind contributions.

Pakistan has also recently developed ways to support private schools that serve low-income students. The Cluster-Based Teacher Training Program was introduced to improve teaching practices in Punjab by engaging specialists to conduct content knowledge training for teachers in clusters consisting of one public and two private schools. Similarly, the Quality Assurance Certification Program categorizes schools using quality criteria to inform parents' choice among schools while also providing tailored capacity-building programs in public and private schools (LaRocque 2008).

The private sector can introduce efficiencies in public education management. Private organizations can advise public schools in pedagogical and management issues for a specified period of time, under contract stipulations and with the possibility of transferring the school back into public management. When a private contractor provides schools with technical assistance and has the ability to influence school decision-making, this can help reduce inefficiencies and thus improve the management of the school.

In Pakistan, Punjab's Directorate of Education has contracted with Idara-e-Taleem-o-Agahi, a Lahore-based NGO, to serve as a temporary technical adviser on pedagogical and human resources matters under an adopt-a-school program. The period of engagement is one year to carry out the core work of the contract and an additional two to three years to transfer back these responsibilities to the directorate. Through a memorandum of understanding, the organization took over failed public schools and agreed to transfer knowledge and skills in planning, budgeting, education management information systems, and pedagogy to the schools' managers (Sarwar 2006). This approach addresses the weaknesses of traditional adopt-a-school programs, in which a private sector organization donates money or makes other contributions (such as volunteer staff time) but with no binding agreement between the parties that gives the private organization authority over key aspects of school management.

Alternatively, schools can contract with private organizations to provide a package of services that may include, for example, management training for principals, educational materials, teacher training, and technology services. In Brazil, public and private schools subscribe to the Pitagoras Network, and receive integrated advice on management procedures and pedagogic methods through yearly contracts for a cost equivalent to the cost of buying a set textbooks for every pupil (Rodriguez and Hovde 2002). Aligning the three core pedagogical elements (curriculum, teacher training, and pedagogic techniques) with school management is one of the strengths of Pitagoras's services towards quality improvement (Rodriguez and Hovde 2002). Pakistan has a similar program, Aga Khan Education Services, which works with the Directorate of Private Education to strengthen instructional practices and management in low-cost private schools (LaRocque 2008).

Many of the functions traditionally carried out by local education authorities can also be outsourced to the private sector. The United Kingdom authorized the contracting out of local authority functions in 2002 as part of a reform to introduce market dynamics into the education system. Local education authorities are responsible for funding and managing state school services for a local area (Hatcher 2006), but private organizations are contracted by the government to provide education services if the local education authorities are found to be failing in their performance or if they voluntarily decide to outsource these functions for efficiency reasons (LaRocque 2008). The United Kingdom's legislation envisions the new role of local education authorities as brokers between schools and private organizations as opposed to simple service providers (Hatcher 2006). Services such as pedagogic support, curriculum advice, school improvement strategies,

information technology training, and ancillary services can be outsourced, whereas key services such as budget approval cannot. There are an estimated 8,000 education providers in the United Kingdom, and $789 million was spent on private sector consultants in 2002–03 (Hatcher 2006).

Governments can contract with private companies to provide academic support for disadvantaged students. School districts in the United States are required by federal law to provide supplemental education services both to schools that have not made adequately yearly progress for three consecutive years, and to schools with high percentages of poor children (more than 40 percent) or students with special needs (Burch, Steinberg, and Donovan 2007). These supplemental services include after-school tutoring, remediation, and other academic support activities that take place outside regular school hours (United States Department of Education 2007). As a result, the number of students receiving supplemental education services increased from 117,000 in 2004–05, to 430,000 in 2005–06 (General Accounting Office 2006), and the supplemental services industry grew by an average of 14 percent annually between 2000 and 2003 (Hentschke 2005). The program requires private providers to offer high-quality and research-based services, and imposes few barriers to entering the market (Burch, Steinberg, and Donovan 2007).

While theoretically, this U.S. initiative is designed to encourage competition between providers and increase the access of low-income students to high-quality academic support, critics argue that larger firms have so far been in a better position to acquire greater market shares, hence undermining competitiveness. Other criticisms that have been voiced are that providers have few incentives to serve special needs students because of the high cost of providing this kind of education (Burch, Steinberg, and Donovan 2007), that it is too difficult to monitor and evaluate the service providers effectively (most evaluations are based on school visits and self-reports rather than performance indicators), and that providers have to deal with complicated contracting requirements (General Accounting Office 2006).

The private operation of public schools

Governments can also contract out the entire school operation, including the education of students, school management, financing, staffing, the provision of professional services, and building maintenance. One argument in favor of publicly funded but privately managed schools is that they have the potential to improve quality and increase efficiency because they have more autonomy than traditional public schools, which means that they are subject to fewer constraints such as bureaucratic requirements and pressure from teachers' unions (Gill et al. 2007; Hatcher 2003). In addition, in schools that are publicly funded but privately managed, decisions about school management are made at a level that is closer to the beneficiary than in other public schools (World Bank 2003a). When governments make such operation contracts with private organizations, they are leveraging not only the organization's expertise but also its innovative instructional and management practices. Publicly funded private schools can transform the education system from the outset, simply by providing a wider range of schooling alternatives. Moreover, because they must offer free education and enable school choice, they provide additional places for students who are traditionally under-served.

With its highly decentralized education system and an active capital market that invests in for-profit education management organizations and institutions that channel funds to education businesses, the United States is the country with the most experience with contracting out the operation of public schools to the private sector (Hatcher 2006).

There are two kinds of private management of schools in the United States—managed schools and charter schools. The first kind exists when school districts allow Education Management Organizations, for-profit firms authorized to manage schools receiving public funds, to take over public schools, usually failing ones, managed by school districts or charter holders (Molnar et al. 2006). Managed schools operate in 29 U.S. states and increased from 135 in 1998–99, to 521 in 2005–06 (Molnar et al. 2006). The second kind of private management involves charter schools, which are public schools that have been contracted out to a private operator for management purposes. In 2007–08, there were 4,147 charter schools in 40 U.S. states, up from 253 in 1995–96 (Center for Education Reform 2007). Because of the decentralized nature of the education system in the United States, the degree of autonomy varies by state.

In the United Kingdom, academies are independent schools operated by an autonomous private consortium in partnership with the central government and local education stakeholders. The government provides most of the funding for these academies, with the private consortium expected to contribute 20 percent. The academies are free from any regulations imposed by local education authorities regarding education and staffing issues. The consortium can engage in trade (to accumulate funds from private or public sources) to generate profits for the academy (OECD 2004b). Similarly, the government of Qatar introduced the Independent School Program in 2004 as part of a decentralization reform aimed at transferring the management of all public schools to independent operators by 2011, at introducing school accountability, and at boosting academic performance. Private operators either revamp weak public schools or establish new schools (Brewer et al. 2007).

Latin America has two examples of privately managed public schools. The first is Venezuela's Fe y Alegría network, which provides free education to poor communities in under-served areas and receives funding (85 percent of the operational costs) from the government through an agreement between the Ministry of Education and the Venezuelan Association of Catholic Education. Fe y Alegría schools account for 8 percent of total enrollments in Venezuela (Allcott and Ortega 2007).

Concessions schools in Colombia are the second example. This concept was introduced by the government in 1999 as a way to provide high-quality education to low-income and high-risk students (Barrera-Osorio 2007). Concession schools are public schools managed by private school operators with a record of scoring above-average on the national secondary exit examination for five consecutive years. Private operators are granted autonomy over school management and receive a per pupil payment. In Bogota, there are 25 public schools run as concession schools under 15 year contracts (Villa and Duarte 2005). The program sought to overcome the limitations of some demand-side programs, such as the lack of a requirement to demonstrate improved outcomes before being allowed to continue receiving public funds, by requiring concession schools to score above-average on the annual national academic test (Villa and Duarte 2005).

Privately operated schools have more autonomy than traditional public schools to introduce innovations and to make their own decisions about staffing, curricula, and pedagogical methods as long as they follow national labor laws and national academic standards. For instance, Fe y Alegría schools are considered to be successful in improving education outcomes because of their decentralized and autonomous nature, which has been replicated in other Latin American countries (Allcott and Ortega 2007). Privately operated schools provide a free education but also allow school choice, thus encouraging competition between schools and more parental accountability in similar ways as voucher programs (box 2.3).

School operators are granted contracts for a fixed term, ranging from three (United States) to fifteen years (Colombia). These contracts stipulate clear responsibilities and objectives, and can allow governments to collect information on education indicators that can be used to assess school performance (World Bank 2003a). Contracts also include cancellation guidelines if school operators fail to meet education, performance, or management benchmarks (Fitz and Beers 2002). For instance, in Colombia, contracts stipulate that concession schools must score above average on national standardized tests. Moreover, these schools must adhere to many of the regulations

---

BOX 2.3   *The differences between charter schools and vouchers: The case of the United States*

In the United States, charter schools give parents a choice among schools as vouchers do, but there are three main differences between these two systems:

- A governmental body must approve the establishment and continued operation of a charter school, while schools educating voucher students do not need explicit permission to operate.

- Charter schools are not allowed to promote religion, while schools educating voucher students often have a sectarian affiliation.

- Charter schools are accountable for the academic results of their students on state and federal tests, whereas schools educating voucher students are not.

Source: Gill et al. 2007.

---

that apply to public schools, such as those related to pupil-teacher ratio and minimum pass rates, and must subscribe to centrally determined academic standards.

The fact that private operators can be for-profit, not-for-profit, or community organizations sets incentives to attract highly qualified organizations to run failing public schools. For instance, in an attempt to diversify the education market, the Qatari government sought to attract a variety of potential operators of independent schools, including foreign education management companies, by allowing them to make a reasonable profit to operate several schools at once to realize economies of scale (Brewer et al. 2007).

The *World Development Report 2004* (World Bank 2003a) discusses the lack of systematic learning from innovations and insufficient replication of successful practices. Contracting out the operation of schools to the private sector can reverse this problem by building incentives into the contracts that encourage operators to replicate and scale up good practices. The good practices to be replicated should be identified either through local research or through statistical analysis.

Private sector involvement in building school infrastructure

The United Kingdom's private finance initiative allows partnerships consisting of private consortiums and public authorities to construct and maintain education facilities. The increased interest in private finance initiatives shown by governments in recent years has been accompanied by substantial growth in the global pool of capital available for investment in infrastructure. Infrastructure funds manage an estimated $133 billion worldwide, 77 percent of which was raised between 2006 and 2007 (Palter, Walder and Westlake 2008).

There are three main arguments in favor of private finance initiatives. First, these arrangements enable governments to attract private investment, which benefits those whose public resources for infrastructure are declining (HM Treasury 2008). Second, the private partner takes on a share of the responsibility and risk for the infrastructure project as a condition of the contract (PricewaterhouseCoopers 2005). Third, there is a fiscal incentive to circumvent regular budgeting procedures because only the annual rents that the government pays to the private contractor are deducted from the annual budget instead of the entire amount of the investment (Sadka 2006). From an education perspective, private finance initiatives help governments to provide appropriate school buildings and to relieve teaching staff and school administrators of maintenance duties that are outside of the primary scope of their work, allowing them to concentrate on meeting the learning needs of students.

The United Kingdom leads the world in infrastructure PPPs, with 10 to 15 percent of its public sector capital investment made through private finance initiatives (International Financial Services London 2008). Education projects account for about 19 percent of infrastructure private finance initiative contracts and 8.5 percent of their value (LaRocque 2008). Recent increases in the amount and value of its deals make it clear that the government heavily emphasizes this procurement delivery model. As of 2008, private finance initiatives in education attracted capital investment totaling $11.6 billion, and this is projected to increase to $16 billion by 2010 (HM Treasury 2008).

Australia's first PPP infrastructure program, which ended in 2005, built nine schools in New South Wales for $129 million. The success of this experience led to a second round of the program in which 10 schools are to be completed between 2006 and 2009 for $168 million (The Audit Office of New South Wales 2006). Three other provinces, Queensland, South Australia, and Victoria, are in the early stages of contracting with private consortiums to finance, build, design, repair, and maintain school buildings, but leaving the provision of education to public authorities (LaRocque 2008).

The Egyptian government has signed 15- to 20-year contracts with private partners to design, finance, and maintain 300 schools in 23 governorates and expects to expand the initiative to 2,210 schools by 2011 (LaRocque 2008). Several European countries are also adopting this procurement procedure. Belgium's Flanders province approved a PPP project that will select a single consortium to finance, construct, and maintain all schools built under private finance initiatives in order to benefit from economies of scale (OECD 2006). Germany has engaged in a private finance initiative to renovate, maintain, and manage 90 schools in the Offenbach province for 15 years as well as an initiative to refurbish and operate seven schools in Cologne for 25 years (LaRocque 2008). Also, the Canadian province of Alberta has authorized 32 PPP fixed-price contracts for 30 years, under which the private contractor assumes the risks of the costs of inflation and of any construction delays (LaRocque 2008).

Most of the evidence about school facility PPPs come from the United Kingdom, where a focus on due diligence has kept the number of projects exceeding time and cost estimations to a minimum and where the private lenders' assumption of risk has reduced the government's losses when initiatives have failed (PricewaterhouseCoopers 2008). In 2003, 73 percent of construction projects under traditional procurement in the UK exceeded the contract price, and 70 percent were delivered late. In comparison, only 22 percent of projects under private finance initiatives exceeded the contract price, and only 24 percent were delivered late (PricewaterhouseCoopers 2008). Similarly, a strong emphasis on analyzing and allocating risk has increased discipline in procurement (PricewaterhouseCoopers 2008). However, critics have argued that the design and eventual construction of private finance initiative schools is of low quality, that users were not always satisfied with specific aspects of the building, and that there is no evidence that private finance initiatives are less expensive than traditional direct government financing (United Kingdom Audit Commission 2003).

The literature is consistent in emphasizing that the main reason to adopt private finance initiatives is value for money, which can be defined as the optimum combination of service quality and cost (over the whole life of the contract) to meet user demands. However, this does not necessarily imply lower costs (HM Treasury 2008). A better way to estimate value for money is by comparing the net present value of private finance initiative proposals with public sector benchmarks that represent the cost that the government would otherwise have incurred in the procurement project (Hurst 2004).

Ireland's public sector benchmarks are not public, so there is no evidence that private finance initiatives were better values than direct public financing. In fact, they may have been more expensive given the high costs of private financing and of the tendering process (Hurst 2004). In Australia, the cost of the public sector comparator exceeded the net present cost of the private sector by $9.8 million in the first round of the New South Wales project and by $48.8 million in the second (Audit Office of New South Wales 2006). The savings were partly due to the economies of scale achieved by assigning the management of nine schools to one private contractor, a clearly defined business case proposal, a competitive tender process, and sound performance and evaluation systems (OECD 2004a).

While one of the main advantages of infrastructure PPPs was to enable governments to avoid reporting the entire cost of the infrastructure project in the budget at one go, the United Kingdom government recently announced that infrastructure PPPs must follow international financial reporting standards, which means that future private finance initiative contracts

must be recorded on the books (PricewaterhouseCoopers 2008). This reduces governments' fiscal incentive to use private finance initiatives, leaving only the long-term incentives for good performance and increased discipline in contracting that PPPs encourage (PricewaterhouseCoopers 2008). The rationale for recording both the incremental payments and the potential future costs of PPPs in fiscal accounts is to assure transparency, ensure debt sustainability, and conduct appropriate fiscal planning (IMF 2004). Moreover, abiding by accounting standards reduces the possibility that expenditure controls can be bypassed and reduces hidden costs relative to traditional procurement (IMF 2004). Very few private finance initiatives are kept off the books in Australia, and this demonstrates that a robust PPP policy and fiscal accountability are possible (PricewaterhouseCoopers 2008).

Nonetheless, private finance initiative procurement is contentious. The primary criticism is that the high interest rates charged by commercial banks to private borrowers for infrastructure make the initiatives more expensive for governments (Jones, Vann and Hayford 2004). This is because banks think that the government's ability to rely on tax revenues if a project fails means that it will not default on the loan (PricewaterhouseCoopers 2008). While this ability does exist, it is an inappropriate criterion by which to evaluate private finance initiatives because it does not consider that public borrowing must ultimately be funded by taxpayers or that the sustainability of public debt depends on the ability of taxpayers to bear it. In other words, if a government has reached its prudent level of borrowing, a private finance initiative can be a useful way to avoid increasing the public debt, even though the cost of private financing is higher than public borrowing (PricewaterhouseCoopers 2008).

Another argument in favor of private financing relates to the opportunity cost of investing in infrastructure projects. A government can choose not to use its available funding for infrastructure projects because it forgoes the opportunity to buy investments in a broad capital market portfolio and to earn returns equivalent to other investors, thus capitalizing on the advantage of the lower cost of public funding (PricewaterhouseCoopers 2008).

A key characteristic of private finance initiatives is that the private sector is involved in delivering services and sharing risk beyond the construction phase (HM Treasury 2008). Private contractors expect a return in exchange for accepting risk and managing a project (HM Treasury 2008). Public authorities will, in all cases, assume an important part of the risk by placing a high value on the service to be provided if facility construction is delayed or of poor quality. In other words, governments have an interest in guaranteeing the infrastructure needed to provide high-quality education for all. Contracts are critical for properly allocating risk between private and public sectors, but the challenge is to do so in such a way as to create the right incentives for the private sector to deliver the desired outcomes at an optimal price (Hurst 2004). Some examples of projects that have failed in this regard are schools in Belfast, Brighton, and Clacton in the United Kingdom that were forced to close before the contract was completed due to insufficient enrollment, leaving public authorities with heavy financial commitments (House of Commons Education and Skills Committee 2006–07).

Alternatives to conventional systems of public education

Publicly funded private schools can be an improvement over traditional public systems because new operators have autonomy over the selection and implementation of their educational strategies, thus leading to innovation and experimentation. In addition, contracts for operational service tend to attract a wide range of private partners that diversify the supply of education. The governments of Colombia, Qatar and the United States have explicitly pursued this goal and have created incentives to attract high-performing or specialized education organizations to drive up quality, diversify the supply, and increase choice. In Colombia, organizations bidding to run concession schools had to demonstrate that they

already operated education institutions that scored above the average in national examinations, which has led to concession schools having different observable characteristics, such as better infrastructure and academic achievement outcomes, than neighboring public schools. In Qatar, the government received proposals from international as well as national bidders and allowed them to make a reasonable profit as an incentive to run independent schools.

Many of the PPP models involve a transfer of decision-making power to the school, thus making providers directly accountable to the users of the service and increasing their efficiency (World Bank 2007a). One explanation behind the success of privately operated public schools in increasing academic achievement rates, despite spending the same or less money per pupil than public schools, is their greater autonomy over decisions about pedagogical methods and financial and human resources management (Allcott and Ortega 2007; Barrera-Osorio 2007). Ladd (2003) adds the caveat that making individual schools accountable to their consumers may cause inequity because they tend to select better qualified students, who are cheaper to educate, and because incentives to reduce operational costs and to attract more students may prompt them to pursue profit at the expense of educational quality. Although the charter school system requires open enrollment and free education, schools are allowed to adopt tailored curricula that target specific populations, such as likely dropouts or students with a particular interest (Hoxby and Rockoff 2004), which may generate student selection at different levels.

Conclusions

Theory suggests that PPPs can increase access and improve quality in education in a number of ways: (i) by allowing school choice, (ii) by putting competitive pressure on private schools to remain in the market, (iii) by making school operations more flexible, (iv) by setting quality-driven output specifications, and (v) by ensuring an optimal level of risk-sharing between the public and private sector (Patrinos 2000). Public funding of private schools is justified by the argument that poor students will benefit from the opportunity to enroll in private schools of superior quality than the public schools that would otherwise be their only option. Studies demonstrate that private schools are more effective than traditional public schools in delivering higher-quality education outcomes in India, Indonesia, Pakistan, and Tanzania (Andrabi et al. 2007; Bedi and Garg 2000; Cox and Jimenez 1991; Muralidharan and Kremer 2006). However, ensuring academic quality in education systems in which the public sector funds private schools and service operators remains a challenge. International experience with PPPs yields five recommendations.

- Contracts for education services should include output measures and quality indicators to track the progress of the contractors in improving quality and increasing school efficiency. These performance indicators can be quantitative, such as standardized tests or enrollment figures, and/or qualitative, such as school and parental surveys and school inspections (World Bank 2006). Evidence from Colombia shows that for contracts to be effective, education authorities must have sufficient capacity to carry out monitoring and evaluation, perform periodic reviews of school performance, and enforce compliance with the contract's quality measures (World Bank 2006).

- Operating requirements and performance standards should be defined for private schools and operators. Belgium and New Zealand require private schools that receive public funding to meet eligibility criteria (including infrastructure and staff requirements), follow national core curricula, and meet performance benchmarks.

- Innovation and quality improvements should be rewarded to prevent schools from reverting to negative practices, such as lobbying for extra funding, in cases where competition for students results in reduced public funding (Gauri and Vawda 2004). For example, Pakistan's Foundation Assisted Schools Program has an incentive and sanction component that rewards schools with monetary awards for good performance and revokes their subsidies if they are operated poorly.

- The efforts of private schools to improve the quality of their education should be supported, and governments should therefore consider adding capacity-building components to voucher programs. Some private schools may lack the capacity to improve education quality because of unqualified teachers, a shortage of resources to enhance materials and textbooks, and inadequate knowledge of effective teaching techniques and management processes. Some of the support that has been given to private schools to overcome this problem includes facilitating their access to capital and arranging preferential loans to improve infrastructure and buy other critical inputs, as in the case of Mauritius. Contracting out technical assistance to enhance financial management, instructional delivery, and school leadership has been tried in Colombia and Pakistan.

- In some countries, special agencies have been created to manage private school operations and the flow of funds from the government to privately run public schools, and to enforce qualifying criteria and regulations. Examples include the Sindh Education Foundation and the Pakistan Education Foundation in Pakistan, both of which are government agencies that manage PPPs in education and channel funds to private schools. Another example is the Private Secondary School Authority in Mauritius, which is an enforcement agency that oversees the operation of private schools and manages disbursement grants (Mohadeb and Kulpoo 2008). The advantage of specialized PPP agencies is that they may concentrate expertise on education PPPs and centralize the management of contracts and fund transfers, thus promoting greater efficiencies in the interactions between public and private entities.

Spotlight on Chile

The case of Chile provides an example of a universal voucher scheme that presents mixed evidence of the impact of public-private partnerships in education.

In the 1980s, Chile introduced a universal voucher system with the objective of making the education system more efficient. The reform enabled students to select the school of their choice, either public or private, and tied per-student public funding to school enrollment. The rationale behind this policy was that student choice would encourage school competition and increase accountability at the local level by making schools responsive to parental preferences. The provision of public funding to private schools led to the development of a school market in which more than 20,000 new private schools were created and private enrollment rates increased from 32 percent of all enrollments in 1985 to 51 percent in 2005. In 2007–08, approximately 94 percent of all schools in Chile, of which 36 percent are private, received voucher funding.

Nonetheless, empirical research indicates that more than 20 years of reform did not lead to improvements in average academic achievement. Moreover, there is evidence of the existence of student segregation by socioeconomic level and a public-private gap in academic performance that favors those students who were able to transfer from public to private subsidized schools. As it turns out, public schools in Chile did not have a strong incentive to compete, as very few of them were closed despite declines in their enrollment rates. On the other hand, private schools responded to competition by exercising their ability to attract and select students. Recent research shows that private subsidized schools have an academic advantage, which seems to be associated with their ability to select the most able students and those with a greater ability to pay. The beneficiaries of the reform—those who were able to transfer to private schools during the basic education cycle (or "switchers")—have had higher labor market returns to schooling investments than their peers who continued in public schools. The switchers mostly belonged to the middle class and had better cognitive skills than their peers who remained in public schools. On the positive side, there is some evidence of improved household welfare due to parents being able to select the school of their choice based on their revealed preferences and the government's policy of targeting the poorest schools to improve their educational quality.

However, more recent evidence shows that after years of stagnation, results may be improving. Chilean students demonstrated significant improvements in their reading performance in the Program for International Student Assessment (PISA) test between 2000 and 2006, making them the top Latin American country participating in PISA, and ranking just behind Turkey in the overall list of participants. In reading, for example, Chile increased its score by 33 points, equivalent to 0.3 of a standard deviation, although it could be argued that this improvement was driven by the more able students. The Chilean experience suggests that it may take some time for school choice policies to yield improvements in average academic achievement. The government is currently introducing policies that address the problem of student segregation, including preferential subsidies to increase options for students from poor families and the elimination of student selection by subsidized schools. New agencies are being established to take responsibility for setting national standards, tracking student progress, and enforcing regulations relating to schools' academic performance. The gap between the theory and the practice of school choice still needs further exploration. Open access to information has made it possible to analyze the effects of the Chilean experience; this is another lesson from which other countries can learn.

Sources: Hsieh and Urquiola 2003; McEwan et al. 2008; Patrinos and Sakellariou 2008; Contreras et al. 2008; OECD 2007; World Bank 2008.

What Do We Know about Public-Private Partnerships in Education?

chapter 3

In chapters 1 and 2, we have shown that public-private partnerships in the provision of education are growing rapidly in several countries. Unfortunately, there are still few empirical evaluations of these experiences. This chapter presents the results of the rigorous empirical studies of these partnerships and discusses their strengths and weaknesses.

We selected which studies to examine based on how they overcame the problem of self-selection—by students, families, or schools—in most PPP programs. Self-selected beneficiaries may have different characteristics than those who do not apply to or do not benefit from the program. Consequently, simply comparing an outcome (for instance, dropout rates or test scores) between beneficiaries and nonbeneficiaries will not accurately reflect the impact of the program because any observed difference between these two groups may be driven not only by the program itself but also by the initial differences in the observable and unobservable characteristics of the two groups.

Evaluations of voucher programs, one common type of PPP, have to deal with the problem of endogeneity. Voucher programs usually require students to apply, but the students who apply are likely to be better informed or more motivated than their peers. Comparing, for instance, school enrollment rates of recipients and nonrecipients may not accurately reflect the impact of the program because differences in enrollment rates may be due to these inherent differences in characteristics and not due to the actual efficacy of the program (Nechyba 2000; Epple and Romano 1998).

Based on chapter 2's definition of PPPs and four different types of contracts—vouchers, subsidies, the private management of schools, and private finance initiatives—in this chapter we discuss PPP programs in the light of four main objectives—access, quality, cost, and inequality. The ways in which the different types of PPPs can affect education outcomes are briefly discussed. As the definitions of the four types of contracts show, PPPs are complex interventions, and their effects can be numerous and difficult to measure.

The definition and objectives of public-private partnerships

PPPs can be defined as a contract that a government makes with a private service provider to acquire a specified service of a defined quantity and quality at an agreed price for a specified period (Taylor 2003). This definition covers several different types of contracts, which may procure different services and vary in complexity. The services include education services (management, maintenance, and support services like transportation); operation services, such as pure management; and infrastructure (in what is often referred to as a private finance initiative) (LaRocque and Patrinos 2006). This review of the empirical literature focuses on three types of education services and operations—vouchers, subsidies, and the private management of schools—and private finance initiatives for school construction.

Education operations contracts are generally complex. The delivery of education can be measured as the number of students enrolled in any given school, but the number of students attending school does not in itself mean that the students are learning anything. Observing the inputs associated with these contracts is extremely difficult. Moreover, how much students learn depends heavily on their family background, a factor that the school cannot control. In short, the parameters of these contracts are difficult to establish and usually require long-term commitments.

Construction contracts are complex as well. The private provider has to commit to investing over several years, and contracts have to stipulate who owns the infrastructure. These contracts are often build-operate-transfer contracts, which implies an eventual transfer of infrastructure from the private to the public sector. Construction contracts also require a long-term commitment from both partners.

Each type of contract works differently depending on the technical capacity and the rule of law that prevail in a country. Less complex contracts can work more efficiently in low-capacity countries, while more complex contracts require a higher degree of legal and technical development.

Contracting as a means of increasing the private sector's role in education can have several benefits over the traditional public delivery of education. These benefits include greater efficiency, increased choice, and wider access to government services,

particularly for people who are poorly served by traditional methods. Increased private involvement in education, through contracting or vouchers, has the additional advantages of bringing specialized skills to bear in the operation and management of public schools and of circumventing the inflexible salary scales and work rules that tend to prevail in public sector employment.

The final objective of PPPs is to increase the enrollment rates and improve the education outcomes (such as standardized test scores and dropout rates), particularly of students from low-income families. From the government's point of view, reducing costs alone can be an important objective. Table 3.1 presents information on the strengths of the four types of contracts analyzed in this chapter—vouchers, subsidies, private management, and private finance initiatives—with regard to the four main objectives of PPPs: increasing enrollment, improving education outcomes, reducing inequality, and reducing costs.

In terms of enrollment, vouchers and subsidies can in theory deliver very significant positive outcomes as long as there is an adequate private supply of school places. However, these contracts may also reallocate students between public and private schools, and therefore, the net gain in enrollment can be small. Private

Table 3.1   Expected effects of different public-private partnerships on four main education objectives

Contract	Effect on increasing enrollment	Effect on improving education outcomes	Effect on reducing education inequality	Effect on reducing costs
Vouchers	Strong: number of students who receive the voucher	Strong: school choice	Strong when targeted	Strong when private sector is more efficient
Subsidies	Strong: use of already built private infrastructure	Moderate: limited by available places and quality of service delivered in the private sector	Strong when targeted	Moderate
Private management and operations	Moderate: limited by the supply of private school operators	Moderate: limited by available places in the private sector	Strong when targeted	Moderate
Private finance initiatives	Moderate: limited by financial constraints	Low	Strong when targeted	Strong

Sources: Authors' compilation based on World Bank 2003a, 2006; Harding 2002; Latham 2005; LaRocque and Patrinos 2006.

management and private finance initiatives require partners to make large initial capital investment in the construction of schools, limiting their ability to produce substantial changes in enrollments.

Vouchers, subsidies, and private operations, in theory, can have significant effects on education outcomes as discussed further in the next section. In contrast, private finance initiatives can only influence education outcomes to a limited extent because the link between infrastructure inputs and education outcomes is weak: changing only infrastructure—without changing the pedagogic methods and teaching—will have little or no effect on final outcomes (Hanushek 2003).

Equity is an important consideration in the design of PPPs. There are those who fear that increased choice will benefit only better-off and better-informed families, even if the program is ostensibly targeted to the poor. Better-informed families, it is argued, know which schools have the best outcomes and facilities and are, therefore, the best option for their children. In other words, school choice may result in students from more privileged homes becoming segregated in the best schools, thereby further improving their own outcomes, while other students are left behind in ever-deteriorating schools (Fiske and Ladd 2000). Nonetheless, several programs reviewed in chapters 1 and 2 explicitly target low-income students, families, and communities, and all contracts can have a clear redistributive objective as long as targeting is part of the agreement between the public and private sectors. Clearly, this feature of these contracts has to be carefully monitored by the public sector to avoid the segregation effect.

Some evidence suggests that the private sector delivers high-quality education at low costs around the world. Indeed, the correlation between the private provision of education and high values for indicators of education quality is positive. Using data from the OECD's Programme for International Student Assessment (PISA), Woessmann (2005) showed that public schools produce lower test scores than privately managed but publicly funded schools do. As a result, partnerships between the private

sector (as the operator of schools) and the public sector (as the financier of schools) can increase enrollment while keeping the education budget low. With regard to private finance initiatives, the major argument in their favor is cost savings. The cost savings generated by the other types of contracts depend on the specifics of the contract (for example, the face value of the voucher) and the private sector's effectiveness in delivering the service.

Intermediate effects and final outcomes

PPP programs affect school outcomes in two different ways. First, PPP programs can be expected to affect how schools function internally and, specifically, how they allocate their resources. Second, students and their families are likely to react to the new incentives that are inherent in, for example, voucher programs, leading to a reallocation of students among schools.

The theoretical literature on the topic suggests that there are four ways in which the private provision of public services affects educational outcomes (see LaRocque and Patrinos 2006; Savas 2000; Nechyba, 2000; Epple and Romano 1998). Each study analyzed certain critical variables to assess the actual effect of a PPP program on education outcomes. The following four conclusions may apply slightly differently to each of the four kinds of PPP contract— private management, vouchers, subsidies, or private finance initiatives:

1. PPP contracts give schools more flexibility in how they manage and provide education services than the public sector alone does. Generally, the public sector gives schools very little flexibility in hiring teachers and organizing schools, so a flexible PPP contract can make it possible for schools to create a better fit between supply and demand.

   Two of the school's management decisions are critical—how teachers are hired and how the budget is allocated. In general, schools operating under a PPP contract have more freedom in teacher hiring and firing than public schools do. Also, private schools can give their administrators more budgetary freedom, which may lead to a more efficient allocation of resources. Finally, schools operating under PPPs have more flexibility in determining such matters as the length of the school day and the length of the academic year.

2. Private providers in PPP contracts are usually chosen through an open bidding process based on quality and cost criteria. Furthermore, the contracts often require contractors to produce certain outcomes, such as increases in test scores. Thus the contracting process and the resulting contract can yield a higher quality of education.

This argument is especially relevant for the private management of public schools. The process by which beneficiary schools are chosen can be transparent and, thus, can be directly observed. Some PPP programs set quality requirements for their contractors. For instance, concession schools in Bogota, Colombia, are based on a bidding process in which the applicant must have previous experience in the education sector (Barrera-Osorio 2007). On top of this, part of the assessment of the applicant's bid includes examining its performance in its other schools based on a national standardized examination. In short, outcomes such as test scores and dropout rates are critical variables to measure in awarding these contracts. As shown below, most studies concentrate on measuring the impact of PPPs on these kinds of outcomes.

3. A PPP contract can achieve an optimal level of risk-sharing between the government and the private sector. This risk-sharing may increase efficiency in the delivery of services and, consequently, may increase amount of resources and improved provision in the education sector.

Measuring the optimal level of risk-sharing is not straightforward. Financial indicators such as revenue-to-cost ratio, revenue-to-student ratio, and cost-to-student ratio can be proxies to measure risk-sharing. In short, to ascertain different risk-sharing options, it is first necessary to examine quantifiable financial indicators.

4. PPPs can promote competition in the market for education. The private sector can compete with the public sector for students. In turn, the public sector can react to that competition by improving the quality of the education that it provides in its schools.

The argument in favor of competition is that if that option is available (for example, in a voucher system), students and families will shop for the schools that provide the best quality of education (Friedman 1955). For competition to thrive, a market for schools must exist and information on the quality of schools must be freely and widely available. However, it is clearly a challenge to measure competition.

Competition implies that a contracting program will also affect nonbeneficiary schools because some students will leave those schools. Ideally, the impact of such a program should be measured by comparing two very similar groups of individuals, one group that benefits from the program (the treatment group), and one group that does not participate in the program, (the control group). These two groups should be similar in terms of both their observable and unobservable characteristics. Since competition implies that the program affects the control group as well as the treatment group, this makes it more difficult to make a meaningful and accurate comparison between beneficiaries and nonbeneficiaries. Data from before and after the start of the program can help to analyze the flow of students between schools. This makes it possible to track students who switch from nonbeneficiary schools to beneficiary schools and consequently to control for these effects.

In general, students who receive vouchers will choose to spend them at a better school than their current one. In the new school, they will interact with students who on average perform better academically than their previous classmates. This interaction can improve the education outcomes of the voucher recipients through peer effects (Nechyba 2000), but this makes it very difficult to disentangle the effects of the voucher itself from the effects of interacting with better students.

In short, there are four factors that can improve education outcomes—flexibility in provision, incorporating quality criteria into the contract, optimal risk-sharing, and competition. Table 3.2 presents the relative strengths of these factors in the four different types of contracts that we discuss in this chapter.

In the case of the private management of schools, flexibility, quality criteria, and higher provider standards play a significant role in ensuring success. Quality criteria seem to be particularly important in these kinds of contracts, which usually give a great deal of flexibility to the private provider. By contrast, risk-sharing plays a minimal role in this kind of contract because the government guarantees a certain amount of resources and the demand for places is usually very strong so the private provider does not face much risk.

In the case of vouchers, the main factors that positively influence education outcomes are quality criteria and competition, as explained previously. Quality control in this case is exercised when parents take their children out of the worst schools and enroll them in the best ones. As long as the parent picks a private school for his or her child, then flexibility seems to play a significant role in improving higher education outcomes. Risk-sharing is not a critical component of this kind of contract.

In the case of subsidies, the most significant factor is the quality criteria. In general, the government establishes certain requirements that must be met by the private schools that receive subsidies. Risk-sharing and competition are of secondary importance for this kind of contract.

Table 3.2 The effects of different types of public-private partnership contracts on education outcomes

Factor	Private management of schools	Vouchers	Subsidies	Private finance initiative
Flexibility	Significant	Moderate	Moderate	Low
Quality criteria	Significant if in the contract	Significant if parent and student driven	Moderate but significant if in the contract	Low
Risk-sharing	Low	Low	Moderate	Significant
Competition	Low	Significant	Low	Low

Source: Authors' compilation.

Finally, in the case of private finance initiative contracts, the most important factor is the risk-sharing agreement between the government and the provider.

Overall, some PPP programs are complex interventions that create incentives that modify several aspects of students' behavior and of school operations. Identifying the ways in which PPPs affect education outcomes is extremely difficult because it requires analysts to disentangle each of these incentives. This is an area in which more study is needed.

Empirical evidence

The main challenge in evaluating PPPs is to overcome the problem of endogeneity, which typically arises because of self-selection.

The challenge is to build the right control group with which to compare the outcomes of the beneficiaries of program. This challenge exists in all impact evaluations, but in education it is exacerbated by the fact that self-selection comes from two sources, schools and students. For instance, in the case of subsidies, schools decide first whether to apply for the subsidy and then students decide which school to attend, based partly on whether the school receives the subsidy. Clearly, schools and students who decide to apply for the subsidy have different characteristics than the ones who choose not to apply.

This section presents empirical evidence of the impact of PPPs along two dimensions: first, by the type of empirical strategy used to tackle the problem of endogeneity, and second, by the type of contract involved in the PPP. Our analysis is limited to those evaluation studies that address self-selection through one of six strategies—randomization, regression discontinuity analysis, instrumental variables, Heckman correction models, difference in difference estimators, and propensity score matching (see appendix B for detailed description of these evaluation methods).

Besides the manner in which endogeneity is addressed, our analysis also takes into account the type of PPP contract used. To this end, this chapter evaluates nine studies of vouchers, three studies of subsidies, four studies of private management contracts, and one study of private finance initiatives. Because we discussed the details of these programs in chapter 2, this chapter focuses only on the results of the studies.

Vouchers

There are numerous studies of the education effects of vouchers, especially in the United States (Gill et al. 2007) but also in other parts of the world (Barrera-Osorio and Patrinos 2009). Table 3.3 briefly summarizes these studies.

Colombia's Programa de Ampliación de Cobertura de la Educación Secundaria was a voucher program launched in large cities in 1991 by the national government. Its main objective was to increase access to secondary education for low-income families, and it assisted 125,000 such students. It targeted neighborhoods classified as falling into the two lowest socioeconomic strata and children who attended public primary schools, offering the families of these children a voucher worth approximately $190 to use at the school of their choice. Families could supplement the value of the voucher if their chosen school charged more than its value, but not all private schools accepted the vouchers. The majority of cities and towns allocated vouchers through a lottery when demand exceeded supply, which enabled Angrist et al. (2002); Angrist, Bettinger, and Kremer (2006); and Bettinger, Kremer, and Saavedra (2008) to evaluate the program using randomization techniques.

Angrist et al. (2002) and Angrist, Bettinger, and Kremer (2006) found that Colombia's voucher program had positive effects on several outcomes over both the short and long term. Recipients of the vouchers attended private schools 15 percent more than nonrecipients did. Beneficiaries had 0.1 more years of education than nonrecipients did as well as lower repetition rates. They were also more likely than nonrecipients to complete the eighth grade, and they scored 0.2 standard deviations higher on standardized tests than nonrecipients did—a significant finding. The evaluations did not identify any short-term effects on enrollment.

In a complementary paper, Bettinger, Kremer, and Saavedra (2008) present evidence in opposition to the hypothesis that vouchers succeed only through peer effects. Moreover, they show that private vocational institutions teach more relevant skills than public voucher establishments do, which confirms the theory that flexibility in school management is a key to better education outcomes.

The evidence on vouchers in Chile is mixed and controversial. Chile's experience dates from the 1980s, and any control group is likely to be subject to competition effects and thus would contaminate the effects of the voucher system (Bellei 2005). Disentangling these effects is difficult, especially because of the lack of randomized assignment and limited baseline information (Hoxby 2003). Presumably, this is the reason why different studies have yielded such different results.

Examples of early studies of the voucher system in Chile include Rodriguez (1988), Aedo and Larranaga (1994), and Aedo (1997). In general, these studies compared the outcomes of beneficiaries with those of nonbeneficiaries and are thus prone to bias in their estimates. A second generation of studies used better data and more sophisticated estimation methods (Bravo, Contreras, and Santhueza 1999; Carnoy and McEwan 2000; Mizala and Romaguera 2000; Vegas 2002). Nevertheless, these studies were still prone to selection bias. Our review of the empirical literature includes the most recent studies of the program's effects on education outcomes, including

Table 3.3 Studies of vouchers

Empirical strategy	Country and study	Data: type and year	Outcome variables	Results
Randomization	Colombia (Angrist, Bettinger, and Kremer 2006)	1999–2001 ICFES (National exam, grade 11) records student level	Standardized test scores (math, reading), completion, cost	Math and reading scores generate a voucher effect of 0.2 standard deviations. Improves test scores for both average students and those over the 90th percentile.
	Colombia (Angrist et al. 2002)	1995; Cross-section, student level	Standardized test scores (math, reading, writing)	Voucher recipients scored 0.2 standard deviations higher than nonrecipients. Voucher recipients' 8th grade completion rates were 10 percentage points higher, and their private school attendance rates were 15 percentage points higher.
	Republic of Korea (Kang 2007)	1995 TIMSS (International test in math and science); Cross-section, student level	Standardized test scores (math), 7th and 8th grades	1 standard deviation increase in mean quality of peers enhances math scores at the 0.25 and 0.5 quantiles by 0.47 and 0.42 standard deviations.
				Students above the 0.75 quantile are not affected by the mean quality of their peers, but weak and median students around and below the 0.5 quantile are strongly affected by it.
Instrumental variable	Chile (Hsieh and Urquiola 2006)	Cross-sections, different sources, 1982, 1970, 1999 TIMSS; student level	Standardized test scores (language, math), 4th and 8th grades; repetition rate; years of schooling; sorting measure of scores	Increase in 1 standard deviation of private enrollment decreases change in sorting measure (language) by 1.21–0.19 standard deviations without pre-trend control for different instrumental variables. When controlling for pre-trend changes in standard deviation, goes in same direction. Same pattern observed when sorting measure is mathematics.
	Chile (Hsieh and Urquiola 2006)	1983–96 SIMCE (National exam, different grades); student level		1 increase in standard deviation of private enrollment increases standard deviation in sorting measure of repetition rate by 0.50–1.62 using different instruments without pre-trend and with pre-trend goes from 0.47–1.71 standard deviations change.
	Chile (Gallegos 2004)	Cross-section, 1994–97, student level	Average of the math and Spanish portions of test scores in 4th and 8th grades	1 standard deviation in private enrollment generates about 0.20 standard deviation in test scores and 0.24 in productivity.
				1 standard deviation of number of priests per person boosts private enrollment by 8 percentage points.
	Chile (Contreras, Bettinger, and Sepulveda 2008)	Cross-section, 2005, student level	Selection of schools (parents' questionnaire), standardized test, math reading and science, 4th grade	After controlling for self-selection, no differences between public and private schools.
	Sweden (Sandström and Bergström 2004)	National achievement test, 1997–98, student and municipal level	No failing grades	Greater competition improves the standards of public schools.
	Netherlands (Himmler 2007)	National data, 2002–03, student level	Secondary school grades, per student spending, grade inflation	Positive link between intensity of competition and academic achievement in secondary school.
Heckman correction model	Chile (McEwan 2001)	Cross-section, 1997, student level	Standardized test scores (language, math) 8th grade	Adjusted differences in test scores between public corporations, Catholic voucher, Protestant voucher, nonreligious voucher, private nonvoucher schools and public schools show differences of –0.16, 0.35, –0.18, 0.002, and 0.62. Similar results emerge for Spanish.
	Chile (Sapelli and Vial 2004)	Cross-section, 1998 and 1999, student level	Standardized test scores, language	Large positive effects; 0.5 standard deviation. Effects not due to sorting or peers.
	Chile (Elacqua, Contreras, and Salazar 2008)	Cross-section, 2002 student level	Standardized test scores, language and math, 4th, 8th, and 10th grades	Franchise schools scores were between 0.20 and 0.50 standard deviation higher than private independent schools. No differences between private independent and public schools.

Sources: Authors' compilation; Barrera-Osorio and Patrinos 2009.

McEwan (2001); Gallegos (2004); Sapelli and Vial (2004); Hsieh and Urquiola (2006); Elacqua, Contreras, and Salazar (2008); Patrinos and Sakellariou (2008); and Contreras, Bustos, and Sepulveda (2008).

Sapelli and Vial (2004) used a Heckman estimation to model parents' decisions to participate in Chile's voucher program. They found that the program had positive effects (a 0.5 standard deviation) on beneficiaries' test scores. By contrast, McEwan (2001) used a similar estimation and found that adjusted differences in math test scores between public schools and different types of private schools—Catholic voucher, Protestant voucher, and nonreligious voucher schools—ranged from 0.02 to 0.31 standard deviations. A recent estimation (Elacqua, Contreras, and Salazar 2008), using the same type of technique and analyzing differences between public schools and two types of private schools (franchises and independent private schools), found no differences between private independent schools and public institutions and a difference of 0.20 standard deviation between franchises and public schools. Patrinos and Sakellariou (2008) found that the main beneficiaries of the 1981 reform were students who were just entering primary school or who were already in basic education.

The issue of sorting—private schools choosing the best students and the best public students choosing private schools—has often been explored in the context of the Chilean voucher program. Contreras, Bustos, and Sepulveda (2008) found that student selection is a widespread practice among private subsidized schools. After controlling for a series of selection criteria and the segmentation effects that they produce, there were no differences in results between public and private subsidized education. A student attending a school that used selection criteria performed 6 to 14 percent better on standardized mathematics tests than a student from a school that did not use selection criteria. Hsieh and Urquiola (2006) used several data sets and instrumental variable approaches to argue that the positive effects of the voucher program are due to sorting. They argued that the best students in public schools used the vouchers to attend private institutions. (Sapelli and Vial 2004, however, presented evidence against the sorting hypothesis.)

Overall, the evidence from the Chilean experience with vouchers presents a mixed picture, with strong empirical support for sorting of students by private subsidized schools.

Studies of education systems in Denmark (Andersen 2005), the Netherlands (Himmler 2007), and Sweden (Sandström and Bergström 2004) that allow for a high degree of school choice, suggest that vouchers have increased competition among schools. Furthermore, in the Netherlands and Sweden, this competition has had positive effects on student achievement.

Private management of schools

The literature on evaluating charter schools in the United States has grown substantially in recent years (see Carnoy et al. 2005 for a comprehensive review and Gill et al. 2007 for a recent review). Table 3.4 summarizes the recent literature. Studies by Booker et al. (2008), Hanushek et al. (2007), Sass (2005), and Solmon (2004) use micro-data from Arizona, Florida, and Texas and apply fixed effects (difference in difference) techniques to reach similar conclusions. Initially, students in charter schools fare worse on standardized tests than their peers in public schools, but after a period of time (usually three years), the scores of charter school students catch up with those of their public school peers. Bettinger (2005), using longitudinal data at the school level, and Bifulco and Ladd (2006), using panel data at the student level, found that charter school students have lower academic scores than public school students.

Hoxby and Rockoff (2004) and Hoxby and Murarka (2007) presented evidence based on randomized interventions. In Chicago, Hoxby and Rockoff (2005) found improvements of 10–11 percentage points in the early grades of charter schools. By contrast, in New York, Hoxby and Murarka (2007) found that the charter school effect was evident in grades 3–8, and was between 0.04 and 0.09 standard deviation.

Barrera-Osorio (2007) and Allcott and Ortega (2007) reached similar conclusions

Table 3.4 Studies of private management

Empirical strategy	Country and study	Data: type and year	Outcome variables	Results
Randomization	United States, Charter schools, Chicago (Hoxby and Rockoff 2004)	Administrative data, cross-section, 2000–2002, student level	Standardized test (math, reading), 1st–8th grades	Positive effects for lower grades: reading, 11 percentile points and math, 10 percentile points. None or a negative impact (–4 percentile points in math) for higher grades (6–8).
	United States, Charter schools, New York (Hoxby and Murarka 2007)	Administrative data, cross-section, 2000–2005, student level	Standardized test (math, reading), 1st–12th grades	Positive effects on math (0.09 standard deviation), reading (0.04 standard deviation), 3rd–8th grades, achievement positively correlated with the length of academic year.
Difference in difference	United States, Charter schools, Texas (Booker et al. 2008)	Administrative data, longitudinal 1995–2002, student level	Standardized test (math, reading), 3rd–8th and 10th grades	Initially (one year), students perform worse in charter schools than in public ones; after three years, students have similar scores to those in public schools.
	United States, Charter schools, Michigan (Bettinger 2005)	Administrative data, panel, school level	Test scores	No statistical differences between (nearby) public schools and charters.
	United States, Charter schools, North Carolina (Bifulco and Ladd 2006)	Longitudinal data, 1996-2002	Standardized test scores (math, reading), 4th–8th grades	Charter students score 0.1 (reading) and 0.16 (math) standard deviation lower than public students.
	United States, Charter schools, Texas (Hanushek et al. 2007)	Administrative data, longitudinal panel, 1996–2002, student level	Standardized test scores (math, reading), 4th–7th grades	Initially, charter students score lower than regular public students (0.17 standard deviation), but this depends on how long the school has been operating; after three years of operation there are no differences between them.
Propensity and matching	Colombia, Concession schools (Barrera-Osorio 2007)	Panel at school level, two years, 1999–2003, student level	Dropout rates, standardized test scores (math, reading), 11th grade	Positive effects on math (0.19 standard deviation), reading (0.27 standard deviation). Positive effects on dropout rates (1.7 percentage points). Some evidence of completion effects on nearby public schools.
	Venezuela, Fe y Alegría (Allcott and Ortega 2007)	Cross-section, 2003, student and school level	Standardized test scores (math, reading), 11th grade	Positive effect on math scores (0.08 standard deviation), verbal (0.1 standard deviation).

Sources: Authors' compilations; Gill et al. 2007.

for Colombia and Venezuela. They found that the private management of schools yielded higher test scores for students at the end of their basic education (grade 11) than public institutions did. These two studies used propensity score matching estimators with limited data and, therefore, their results should be viewed with caution.

Subsidies

There is only limited robust empirical evidence on subsidies (table 3.5). Kim, Alderman, and Orazem (1999) evaluated a subsidy program in Pakistan's Balochistan province. The budget allocation for the program was smaller than the resources needed to cover all the target population.

For this reason, the authorities decide to run a lottery to decide who should benefit. Kim, Alderman, and Orazem (1999) found that the program had had a positive impact on girls' enrollment rates. However, because the baseline treatment and control groups had important differences, it is unclear whether the differences in enrollment between beneficiaries and nonbeneficiaries can be attributed to the program or to other differences in their characteristics.

Uribe et al. (2006) investigated the differences between public and private schools that receive subsidies, especially those concerned with the use of school inputs. They reached several conclusions. First, after controlling for such factors as family background and teacher characteristics,

Table 3.5   Studies of subsidies

Empirical strategy	Country and study	Data: type and year	Outcome variables	Results
Randomization	Balochistan, Pakistan (Kim, Alderman and Orazem 1999)	Panel: baseline and follow-up data, 1994 and 1995, student level	Enrollment rate	Positive impact on girls' enrollment: 22 percentage points (baseline: 56 percent enrollment).
Difference in difference	Bogota, Colombia (Uribe et al. 2006)	School-level panel data, 1999 and 2000, student, teacher, and school level	Standardized test, math, 5th grade	Private and public schools yield the same achievements, after controlling for individual and school characteristics. Private schools have wider dispersion; public schools have teachers with higher level of education. Strong evidence of presence of peer effects. Public schools have larger classes.

Sources: Authors' compilation.

they found that students from private and public schools had similar test scores. Their second finding was that peer effects were one important explanation of higher test scores. Indeed, students with classmates whose mothers had more education had higher test scores. Third, class size was an important determinant of test scores. Fourth, private schools were more flexible in contracting teachers, and teachers in public schools have more education than those in private schools. Fifth, the authors found that the dispersion in test scores in the private sector is wider and that the combination of inputs is more diverse than in public schools.

Private finance initiatives

As discussed earlier, it is not yet clear how upgrading infrastructure affects education outcomes (see table 3.1). Moreover, an important line of research casts doubts on whether increasing inputs such as infrastructure influences education outcomes (Hanushek 2003). The few studies that have assessed the impact of private finance initiatives on education outcomes are case studies; for example, Audit Office of New South Wales (2006) in Australia and Gibson and Davies (2008) in the United Kingdom.

In terms of academic achievement, KPMG (2008) found a significant correlation between private finance initiative schools and improvements in test scores. Essentially, between two rebuilt schools—one

funded by a private finance initiative and the other by the public budget—there is a 90 percent chance that the school whose reconstruction was funded by a private finance initiative will have a faster rate of academic improvement. Moreover, an analysis of the first private finance initiative school in the United Kingdom concluded that the overall impact of the partnership is positive as measured by improvements in the quality of infrastructure, academic performance, students' attitudes and behavior, and attendance indicators (Gibson and Davies 2008). Nonetheless, whether these results will be applicable elsewhere remains to be seen because schools funded by private finance initiatives tend to be characterized by exceptional circumstances such as positive attitudes toward the partnership on the part of both the school and the private contractor that influence the behavior of students and teachers (Gibson and Davies 2008).

The main rationale for private finance initiatives is cost savings. The private sector, with a clear interest in the financial outcomes of its own investments, is more efficient than the public sector in using resources and in maintaining the infrastructure that it builds (Latham 2005). Nevertheless, there is little actual evidence that private finance initiatives lead to cost savings, and, because the model is relatively new, it is difficult to reach firm conclusions.

Channels of impact

It is critical to understand the internal work of schools and how interventions such as PPPs can modify how schools function. Unfortunately, there is little rigorous empirical research on this topic. Uribe et al. (2006) is one of the few attempts to quantify the ways in which PPPs affect education outcomes. Hoxby and Murarka (2007) present some evidence of the relationship between certain traits of charter schools and education outcomes. Also, Bettinger, Kremer, and Saavedra (2008) present evidence on how students acquire skills in private vocational schools. However, all in all, more research is needed on the impact of PPPs on education outcomes.

Conclusions

There is an extensive empirical literature on vouchers that is technically sound. In contrast, the literature on subsidies, private management, and private finance initiatives is less abundant, with most of the evidence on private management consisting of studies of the charter school experiment in the United States. It is critical for researchers to explore further the relationship between PPPs and education outcomes.

Spotlight on Education for All in Africa

In Africa, a region in which the challenge to fulfill the Millennium Development Goals (MDGs) is dire, a dynamic private sector has expanded the access to and quality of education through a variety of public-private partnerships.

In many countries, the private sector plays an important role in the provision of basic education. Traditionally, most nongovernment schools have been faith-based and community-managed schools catering to children from low-income backgrounds, and in some cases, these schools have received public funds. Such is the case in Burkina Faso, where the government funds Catholic and secular private schools, which enroll 35 percent of all secondary school students. Some countries use contracts to outline the respective responsibilities of the public and private sectors in the provision of education, as in Côte d'Ivoire and Uganda.

A worldwide commitment to ensuring universal coverage of basic education has led to public resources being concentrated at the primary level. The increasing flows of students completing primary education resulted in competition for limited places in high-quality public or private-aided secondary schools in many countries, thus giving an advantage to academically superior students. In Kenya, for instance, the transition rate from the primary level to public secondary schools was 57 per-cent with completion rates of only 79 percent. This excess demand for high-quality secondary education resulted in a growth in the creation of low-cost private schools in many countries including Benin and Nigeria. In Lagos, it is estimated that in 2006, 36 percent of total enrollments were in private schools, and these figures may even be an underestimate given the increase in the number of private unregistered schools. In Benin, enrollment rates in private primary and secondary schools increased from 8 to 25 percent between 1990 and 2005.

Increased private sector participation in the provision of education helps governments to absorb student demand. Public perceptions of poor quality education at public schools at all levels are driving the expansion of private schooling. Many of these new private schools cater to low-income families, are for-profit, and charge low fees. The new private providers are aiming to offer a more conducive learning environment than the public schools provide, sometimes with lower pupil-teacher ratios, better infrastructure, and more motivated and account-able teachers. It is estimated that across Africa, 10 percent of students attend nonstate schools and that between 1991 and 2003, the number of private primary schools increased by 113 percent.

Governments are increasingly acknowledging the role that private education plays in improving education quality and widening access. Many of them are devising ways to strengthen the capacity of private schools to deliver high-quality education (for example, by facilitating loans to private schools to improve school infrastructure as in Mauritius and Ghana) and to ensure greater coverage for poor students and developing appropriate regulations to govern the operation of private schools. However, governments still face the challenge of putting in place favorable regulatory environments. It will be crucial for governments to establish clear guidelines for the creation of private schools; set up quality assurance and monitoring processes, and incentive structures; and ensure the free flow of information to parents about their education options.

Sources: IFC 2006; World Bank 2008; UNESCO 2007; Fielden and LaRocque 2008; Verspoor 2008; Lewin and Sayed 2005.

Designing a Conducive Environment for Education Contracting

For public-private partnerships to live up to their potential of bringing many benefits to the education sector, they must be well designed. Poorly designed PPPs can expose governments to significant financial and policy risks, such as cost increases and unmet objectives. Governments can do several things to create an environment that is conducive to the establishment of well-designed and successful PPPs in education, and these are summarized in box 4.1 and discussed in detail in this chapter.

Common weaknesses in education policy and regulations

Positive economic outcomes depend upon the right policies and sound institutions. Well-designed policies are also vital for achieving positive outcomes in the education sector in general and in private education specifically. Box 4.2 presents key principles for effective design and implementation of public-private partnerships in education. The key to ensuring the success of PPPs in education is to put in place an enabling policy and regulatory framework that creates the conditions under which private schools can operate effectively and efficiently. This framework should also ensure that the sector as a whole delivers high-quality education and that the wider public interest is protected.

A key weakness in many countries is government resistance to accepting the private sector as its partner in the social sectors. Thus, while these governments might allow private schools to exist, they do not fully recognize their contribution to achieving important economic, social, and education goals. In addition, many governments limit the number of private schools that can be established and discourage private investment in the education sector. There are many examples of such inappropriate regulation. The most severe are laws that ban private schools outright or fail to recognize their existence. Other weaknesses include unclear and subjective school registration

---

BOX 4.1 *Summary of actions that governments can take to promote public-private partnerships in education*

- Provide a sound basis for the establishment of the private school sector
- Allow private schools to set their own tuition and other fees
- Allow both not-for-profit and for-profit schools to operate
- Promote and facilitate foreign direct investment in education
- Establish clear, objective, and streamlined criteria and processes for establishing and registering private schools
- Provide subsidies to the private school sector

- Ensure that PPP contracts give private providers considerable flexibility
- Establish quality assurance processes and provide families with information to help them to choose schools for their children
- Use a transparent, competitive, and multi-stage process for selecting private partners in PPPs
- Separate the purchaser and provider roles within the education administrative agency
- Ensure that the PPP contracting agency has adequate capacity

- Establish appropriate performance measures and include performance incentives and sanctions for inadequate performance in PPP contracts
- Develop an effective communications strategy to inform parents about school characteristics, and the public about the benefits and objectives of PPPs
- Introduce a framework for evaluating the outcomes of contracts
- Involve international organizations in encouraging the growth of PPPs

BOX 4.2 *Principles for designing and implementing public-private partnerships*

Defining public-private partnerships in education

Principle 1: The nature and extent of PPPs should be based on a government's assessment of its appropriate role in education and the relative costs and benefits of private involvement in the sector, whether this involves education delivery, financing, or regulation.

Principle 2: The equity impact of PPPs should be a key consideration in determining the nature and extent of public and private involvement in education.

Promoting public-private partnerships in education

Principle 3: A sound general policy and regulatory environment, including high standards of public and corporate governance, flexible labor markets, transparency, and the rule of law, including protection of property and contractual rights, are essential for attracting the participation of the private sector in all sectors of the economy, including education.

Principle 4: Authorities can promote private involvement by putting in place an enabling regulatory environment, including recognizing the role of the private education, providing clear and streamlined registration processes, setting up effective quality assurance systems, avoiding regulation of private school fees, and providing incentives for private participation.

Principle 5: Access to capital markets is an essential factor in increasing private participation in education. Restrictions on access to markets and obstacles to international capital movements should be phased out. International organizations can help to promote private sector involvement in education by widening access to capital markets.

Principle 6: Public authorities can promote foreign investment in education by treating local and foreign providers equally, providing investment incentives, and ensuring a supportive and efficient environment for investors. Investment promotion agencies can support investment in education by promoting education as a priority investment sector.

Implementing public-private partnerships

Principle 7: PPP processes should be free of corruption and subject to appropriate levels of accountability, while public authorities should take effective measures to ensure the integrity and account-

ability of all partners and should establish procedures to deter, detect, and sanction corruption.

Principle 8: Education authorities and private organizations should agree on the output- or performance-based specifications to be included in the contract as well as sanctions for nonperformance.

Principle 9: The process for awarding PPP contracts should be competitive and should guarantee procedural fairness, no discrimination, and transparency.

Principle 10: Governments should ensure that the public agencies responsible for forming and overseeing PPPs have the resources, information, and skills required to design, develop, and manage the complex contracting processes. They should ensure that the purchaser and provider roles of the agency are separate; the government can assign responsibility for PPPs to specialized agencies on partnerships and contracting education services if necessary.

Principle 11: Education authorities should have the capacity to identify fraud, track payments, and ensure that subsidies and payment claims are legitimate and accurate. They should also ensure that their private sector partners are paid in a timely fashion.

Principle 12: Public authorities can increase the popularity of PPPs by encouraging informed debate on the role and impact of these partnerships, consulting stakeholders and the public about the use of PPPs, putting in place an effective communications and awareness strategy, and creating a rigorous evaluation program.

Encouraging responsible business conduct

Principle 13: Private partners should observe the principles and standards for responsible business conduct that have been agreed on with the government and should participate in such projects in good faith. They should not resort to bribery and other irregular practices to obtain contracts, nor should they agree to be party to such practices in the course of their infrastructure operations.

Principle 14: Private partners should participate in the government's strategies for communicating and consulting with the public.

Principle 15: Private providers need to be mindful of the consequences of their actions for communities and to work together with public authorities to avoid and mitigate any socially unacceptable outcomes.

criteria and standards, which result in inconsistent and nontransparent application of rules; limits on private schools' ability to set tuition and other fees, or to operate as for-profit entities; foreign investment controls; lengthy and complex school registration processes (box 4.3); limits on private schools' ability to offer alternative curricula and qualifications; enrollment restrictions on private schools; restrictive teacher registration requirements; land-use limits; and onerous requirements on private schools' registration, such as financial prerequisites and ownership of land and infrastructure.

Furthermore, governments generally favor public provision in their funding policies, and this does little to create an environment that enables growth in private education. Over the longer term, this is likely to reduce both the quality and sustainability of the private school sector in developing countries. There are hardly any quantitative measures of the extent to which appropriate regulations foster private education, but one exception is the African private schools investment index, which ranks 36 African countries by how attractive an environment they have created for private investment in education. The index shows that there is much progress to be made in developing more enabling regulatory frameworks, with index scores ranging from only 29 to 68 out of 100 (School Ventures 2008).

Regulations can be an important tool for protecting students from low-quality providers, but they must be well designed. A policy framework that supports the private sector and assures education quality is also key to ensuring the economic and political sustainability of the private education sector in developing countries. Public perceptions of the quality of private education are crucial and can easily be influenced by any adverse publicity about low-quality private providers. This can lead governments to bow to public opinion and reverse their enabling policies, which would adversely affect all providers.

Improving education policy and regulations

There are several different aspects to a policy framework that encourages the growth of private schools in developing countries. The principle behind the framework should be the creation of conditions under which private schools can operate effectively and efficiently, while ensuring that the education that they provide is still of high quality.

Provide a sound basis for the operation of the private school sector

Governments can encourage the expansion of the private school sector by recognizing the important role that the sector plays in providing education. China, Côte d'Ivoire, the Philippines, and Senegal have done this by explicitly recognizing the private sector

---

BOX 4.3 *Registering a private school in Kenya*

Registering a private school in Kenya is a long and complex process. The key steps are as follows:

- The organization or individual that wishes to open a new school submits a registration application to the registrar through the district or municipal education officer along with inspection reports from the public health officer and the inspector of schools, the minutes of the district education board

meeting in which the application proposal was discussed, the certification of registration of the school's business name, the names of the school managers and their education certificates, and proof of land ownership.

- Once the registrar receives the application, he or she presents it to the Ministerial Committee on the Registration of Schools for evaluation.

- If approved, the Committee forwards the application to the Ministry of Education for authorization.

- The Minister of Education authorizes the school to operate.

- The registrar issues a certificate after a final inspection of the school has been conducted by public officials.

Source: Verspoor 2008.

in legislation (LaRocque 1999, 2002; Borja 2003). This recognition can be the foundation for building political and public support for the private sector's involvement in education and for minimizing investor uncertainty. This is particularly important given that education is often seen as a social rather than commercial endeavor.

Allow private schools to set tuition and other fees

Governments can promote private involvement in education by allowing private schools to set their own tuition and other fees. The governments of Ghana, India, the Philippines, and Vietnam limit the level of tuition and other fees charged by independent private schools (private schools that do not receive government subsidies). They also regulate the distribution of tuition and other fees among school owners or require schools to consult the government about any fee increases. While such controls are often aimed at making private education affordable for the poor or preventing price gouging, they can also have negative effects such as causing the quality of education to deteriorate and limiting the profitability of education investments. Even when tuition and other fee limits exist but are not enforced, they can reduce investments by increasing investors' uncertainty. One possible exception is when such limits are agreed as part of a contractual arrangement between the government and a private provider, for example, when the government enters into an education purchase arrangement with a private school for the delivery of education services.

Allow both not-for-profit and for-profit schools to operate

Governments can promote investment in private education by allowing for-profit schools to operate or to receive government subsidies. Several countries ban for-profit providers from the education sector or limit government funding to for-profit private schools. However, this bias against for-profit provision is not universal. Private for-profit schools come in various forms and serve the full range of communities, including elite families, middle-income

families, and poor families. Examples of for-profit school chains include the Beaconhouse Group in Pakistan, the Scholastica Group in Bangladesh, and international providers such as Global Education Management Systems and SABIS. In Pakistan, close to 10 percent of children from families in the poorest socioeconomic deciles were studying in private schools at the end of the 1990s. A recent report by the education NGO Pratham found that rural private schools in India enrolled around 20 percent of all students in India in 2007 (Andrabi, Das, and Khwaja 2006; Srivastava 2007).

Governments often regulate for-profit schools to ensure that they make quality a higher priority than profit. However, that concern should be weighed against the benefits of allowing for-profit schools to operate freely. These include increasing access to education for both poor and nonpoor families, encouraging innovation, and attracting new capital investment and new managerial, pedagogical, and technical skills. The prevalence of private for-profit education worldwide, including private for-profit education that serves the poor, suggests that in practice it has become a valuable alternative to public provision.

Promote and facilitate foreign direct investment in education

Foreign direct investment in education is limited but growing in developed countries, developing economies, and transition economies. In 2005, foreign direct investment in education was nearly $3.5 billion, up from just $86 million in 1990 and $401 million in 2002, and most of it is invested in developed countries (UNCTAD). Foreign direct investment in education remains smaller than in other sectors of the economy. In 2007, it accounted for less than 0.1 percent of foreign direct investment in the service sector (UNCTAD).

Several large-scale private providers operate internationally, including the Academic Colleges Group, the Beaconhouse Group, the Delhi Public School Society, Global Education Management Systems, and SABIS. Religious orders, including the Catholic Church and the Seventh Day Adventist Church, have significant global networks of private schools. These examples show that foreign investment does not flow only from developed to developing countries but in fact much of it is between developing countries or from developing countries to developed countries. This trend is likely to continue given the expansion of education provision in, and the increased globalization of, China and India. In recent years, the governments of both China and Vietnam have encouraged foreign investment to help to meet the growing demand for education in their countries (Borja 2003; VietNamNet Bridge 2006).

Promoting foreign direct investment in education can yield great benefits for the domestic education sector. Foreign private schools can provide families with a wider range of education options, increase competition among schools, and foster innovation. They can also bring in much needed skills, technology, capital investment, and knowledge. By increasing the stock of skilled labor resulting from well-functioning school and higher education sectors, foreign direct investment may improve the investment climate for subsequent foreign investment.

There are several steps that governments can take to promote foreign direct investment in education, including establishing an enabling policy framework within which foreigners can operate schools for both local students and expatriates and providing foreign investors with investment incentives such as tax holidays, subsidies, and land. Governments can also support potential investors by

- providing them with information on investment opportunities in education, the regulatory framework, and the broader investment environment;
- facilitating and simplifying the processing of foreign investment applications;
- setting up an agency to promote education as a target investment sector;
- attending and sponsoring education fairs, exhibitions, and conferences to promote private education investment opportunities;
- proactively seeking to form partnerships with potential investors.

The governments of developing countries can also attract foreign direct investment by providing tax incentives such as exemptions from customs duties on education inputs (books, teaching aids, and information technology equipment) to those companies that invest in the sector. However, while these tax incentives are common in developing countries, the evidence suggests that they have not been particularly successful in attracting investment. This is probably because foreign companies make their investment decisions based on a range of factors including the country's political and macroeconomic stability, the availability of human and natural resources, the state of its infrastructure, and the transparency of its regulatory framework (Tanzi and Zee 2001). Another problem with tax incentives is that they cost governments a significant amount of revenue and, if these costs exceed the benefits, then this is an expensive way to achieve public policy goals. The OECD has prepared a checklist for countries to assess their incentive policies for attracting foreign direct investment (OECD 2003).

Establish clear, objective criteria for establishing and registering private schools

Many countries limit the number of new providers who can set up in the education marketplace. The objective of many of these regulations is to protect consumers from substandard education services, and this is a laudable goal. However, ensuring the quality and safety of private schools and protecting consumers from unscrupulous operators must be balanced against the negative impact of overly restrictive entry criteria, especially in situations where demand for education exceeds what the public sector is able to supply. If the process for registering private schools is convoluted and onerous, then this often has the opposite impact of what the government intended. Rather than promoting increased access, better quality, and safer schools, overly restrictive registration criteria often deter potential providers or increase their costs so much that the newly created schools become unaffordable. Alternatively, these restrictions may prompt some schools to operate outside the law as unregistered or clandestine providers, meaning the government has no way of protecting the affected consumers. The costs of this lack of protection invariably fall disproportionately on the poor, who have fewer education options than others.

To encourage the creation of new private schools and to promote private investment in education, registration criteria for schools should be

- realistic and achievable, so that they do not unduly restrict the establishment of new schools;
- objective and measurable, to limit the scope for corruption;
- open to all prospective private school entrants;
- output-focused, to allow schools to change how they deliver their education services;
- applied consistently across different government levels and departments.

The registration process should not be too long. To avoid unnecessarily long delays, the government could establish performance targets for the regulatory authority and impose time limits on its decision-making. For example, schools could be registered once a certain amount of time had elapsed, irrespective of whether the prospective operator had received official notification from the regulatory authority. The government could also establish one-stop shops (centralized PPP managing agencies) to coordinate the process. The government could also provide potential investors with guidance and information (both on paper and on the Internet) about how to register, including the registration criteria, a detailed description of the process, the registration timelines, and relevant forms.

The government should inform applicants of its decisions in a timely fashion and should include the grounds on which it accepted or rejected the application. There should be a provision in the regulations for provisional registration when certain applicants meet the bulk of the registration requirements. In these cases, the government should inform the applicants of the criteria that they failed to meet and, where appropriate, give them a second opportunity to meet them within a reasonable timeframe. Regulators should not be required to provide provisional registration when the applicant fails to meet a large proportion of the criteria. Instead, these applicants could be required to submit a new, revised application. The process should include an appeal procedure that specifies clear and objective grounds on which those applicants who feel that their application has not been fairly considered may appeal.

Some governments may choose to introduce a graduated registration system for private schools, with provisional registration followed by full registration after a set period. Governments may also choose to grant private organizations, such as private school associations, the power to register private schools or at least to play a greater role in school registration. See box 4.4 for an example of this in Cameroon.

BOX 4.4 *Registering a private school in Cameroon*

Cameroon has a significant private school sector. Private schools are required to be members of whichever private school association is relevant to their school (for example, lay schools or Catholic schools). These associations have several functions, including representing the private sector in policy discussions with the government. In addition, private school associations play a key role in the private school registration process in that they

- work with the prospective private school operator to prepare the application to open a school;
- carry out initial reviews of the application to open a school (including site visits to the school) and recommend any changes needed to improve the school;
- lodge the application with the relevant provincial delegate once complete, along with the private school association's decision whether or not to support the application.

Source: LaRocque and Jacobsen 2000.

Subsidize private schools to encourage investment in education

In addition to providing general investment incentives, governments can encourage private investment in education by offering monetary or in-kind subsidies to private schools. These subsidies can be given at the outset in the form of, for example, free or discounted land, establishment grants, and education infrastructure. Land can be especially important in urban areas where land is expensive. Another way in which governments can encourage private investment would be to facilitate work visas for foreign teachers, management, and technical staff.

Ongoing support can be provided through funding-based PPPs, such as contract schools and charter schools in the United States, concession schools in Colombia, and private school subsidy and voucher programs in both developed and developing countries. Governments can also offer tax credits to parents to cover private school tuition and other fees as an alternative to providing subsidies or give tax benefits to individuals and firms that donate to schools or education trust funds.

These funding-based PPP models all combine government funding with the private delivery of education services. In this respect, they differ fundamentally from both the traditional model of organizing schooling, in which the public sector both funds and delivers education services, and from other forms of PPPs such as Adopt-a-School models, in which the government and the private sector both provide funding and the public sector delivers the education service. Funding-based PPPs support the growth of private education by making it more affordable to families. They are also more effective than alternative funding and delivery models—even fully public and fully private models—in rapidly increasing access to high-quality education because they

- benefit from the much more flexible operating environment in the private sector;
- harness the full range of available public and private resources;
- provide families with the funding that they need to be able to afford private schooling;
- take advantage of the significant network of private schools in many countries to increase access;
- use funding to encourage competition among schools and promote improvements in the quality of education, especially among schools serving low-income families.

Funding-based PPPs can also be a catalyst for the expansion of the private school sector. Kim, Alderman, and Orazem (1999) found evidence that subsidies led to a significant increase in overall enrollments in private schools in poor urban areas (though not in poor rural areas). Similarly, Filer and Münich (2000) found that private schools tended to be established in areas where there was excess demand and where the quality of the state schools was low. In Pakistan, the Punjab Education Foundation's Foundation Assisted Schools Program has expanded rapidly from just 20,000 students in 54 schools in late 2005 to more than 500,000 students in 1,157 schools today (box 2.2 in chapter 2). Also in Pakistan, The Educators, a school franchise model operated by the Beaconhouse Group, has grown to 75,000 students in 230 schools in 130 cities across the country, and 95 low-fee private schools have been established under the World Bank's Balochistan Education Support Project in the first year following the introduction of a voucher-type program.

Funding systems for private schools need to be well designed to ensure that they operate effectively and to minimize corruption. Broadly speaking, governments' school funding systems should be neutral to provide equal treatment to public and private schools, responsive to avoid unnecessary delays in school registration and contracting processes, and targeted to underserved students. While there are many options and designs available for funding-based PPPs, there are several characteristics that they all need to have:

- Public and private schools should be funded in a similar manner, with access to funding based on the quality of the education that the school provides rather than on who owns it.

- The amount of funding provided should be based on student numbers rather than on inputs such as teachers' salaries.
- The funding should be aimed at overcoming the barriers that poor students face in accessing education (for example, funding could be targeted by a student's income or socioeconomic status).
- The funding criteria should be transparent, publicly available, and easily understood.

Governments should make their funding for private schools conditional on the school's satisfactory performance or to its registration and accreditation status to ensure that the funds are allocated to schools with a proven performance record. However, governments should not make the funding conditional on extensive regulation of the schools' inputs and operations as this would limit their ability to run the school in a flexible and responsive manner. It is also important for governments to ensure that these funding programs are well managed and monitored and that they make payments to private schools on a timely basis. This is not the case in many existing programs, for example, in the educational contracting program in the Philippines, where there are long lags between when the students enroll in the school and when the government pays the school its subsidy.

Ensure that private providers have the flexibility to deliver services effectively

For PPPs to be implemented successfully, private partners need to be given considerable flexibility in how they deliver the service for which they have been contracted. The government should spell out the desired outputs and performance standards and set penalties for failure to achieve and rewards for success, but thereafter they should leave it to the providers to decide how best to deliver the required outputs to the specified standard.

Providers must have as much management freedom as possible, especially in staffing and employment as well as in curriculum and budget allocation. To achieve this, governments should adopt operational contracts in which it is specified that the managers of the private school, rather than

the government, will select, employ, and pay school staff. Operational contracts are superior to management contracts because they give the private sector greater flexibility to reorganize work schedules, select appropriately skilled staff, pay the level of salaries required to attract good staff, and dismiss nonperforming staff. Management contracts that put government restrictions on how the contractor operates the school (beyond the minimum standards required to assure safety) can significantly hamper the contractor's ability to determine appropriate resource allocations, introduce management and pedagogical innovations, and improve the quality of education that it delivers.

In operational contracts, the government simply pays the private provider a management fee and an amount per student to operate the school and then allows the provider to make all operational decisions, including those related to staffing. The provider hires all staff, which is particularly important when private providers are expected to improve the performance of failing schools where poor teaching is often a factor. Forcing private providers to operate within the same restrictive regulatory framework that hobbles public schools would significantly restrict the gains from adopting a contracting model and limit the positive impact of competition. Indeed, one recent study found that more than two-thirds of U.S. school district superintendents surveyed believed that reducing bureaucracy and increasing flexibility were very important ways to improve public education (Belfield and Wooten 2003).

Contracts should also reflect the nature of the service provided, encourage private sector investment, and ensure that all risks for nonperformance are covered. Contracts should be contestable—meaning that they are awarded competitively, thus allowing public authorities to compare different offers and select the best provider. Many PPPs involve relatively long-term contracts. For example, private finance initiative contracts are generally for 25–30 years, Bogota concession school contracts are for 15 years, and charter school contracts are for three to five years. Long-term contracts are helpful for giving private partners greater certainty about work stability and thus generate increased interest in education contracts from the private sector. This is especially important given that some governments may easily be persuaded to reverse their policies that favor PPPs given that private education remains controversial. Longer-term contracts also allow contractors more time to achieve their objectives, such as improving school performance.

Less welcome outcomes of longer-term contracts are that they limit some of the benefits of competition, such as the entry and exit of providers in response to changes in demand, and lock in any poorly designed features of contracts for long periods of time. However, these costs need to be weighed against the benefits of increased interest from the private sector and reduced uncertainty for contracted providers. Also, to offset some of these negative effects, some contracts include clauses that require ongoing performance evaluations and the reauthorization of contracts at intermediate points during the contract.

Improve information flows and establish an effective quality assurance system

An important weakness in many countries is the lack of available consumer information on the private education market despite the rapid growth of private education and the wide variations in their price and quality. Many governments collect only limited amounts of information on the fees charged by schools, the programs that they offer, and their staff qualifications, and their regulatory authorities gather little information on the size and nature of the private school and tertiary education sectors. Some countries publish exam scores on a school by school basis (for example, the Philippines and Uganda), while others have adopted innovative ways to provide consumers with information on the performance of schools and tertiary education institutions.

Well-informed consumers and regulators are vital for the successful operation of a market in education. One way to keep consumers informed is to put more stringent requirements on education providers to disclose information about their schools. Among the various ways to make this happen are

- requiring schools to disclose information to regulators and the general public as a condition of registration;
- collecting and disseminating information by education authorities on schools according to a number of indicators, including the quality of their infrastructure, facilities, and curriculum, the qualifications that they offer, and their class sizes, fee levels, teacher qualifications, and exam scores;
- introducing independent school review systems to provide information on school performance, such as the Education Review Office in New Zealand (box 4.5) and the Office of Standards in Education in the United Kingdom;
- introducing independent accrediting agencies that focus on school performance.

BOX 4.5 *New Zealand's Education Review Office*

The Education Review Office is a New Zealand government department responsible for evaluating and reporting to the public on schools, early childhood centers, and other forms of pre-tertiary education in New Zealand.

The office disseminates useful information relevant to parents, educators, managers, and others involved in schools and early childhood education as well as to government policymakers. It reviews individual schools and groups of schools, provides contract evaluation services, and evaluates nationwide education issues. The office publishes national reports that evaluate specific education issues using its inspection evidence.

The Education Review Office schedules reviews of schools and centers based on their prior performance, current risk appraisal, and the amount of time since their last review. Schools are usually reviewed every three to four years, but this can be more frequent if necessary. The office's reports on individual schools and early childhood centers are freely available to the public and can be obtained from the individual school or center or from the Education Review Office itself.

The creation of the office played an important part in supporting the introduction of school choice in New Zealand by providing information on the performance of every school.

Source: New Zealand Education Review Office Web site (www.ero.govt.nz)

Governments might choose to use companies in the private sector that offer testing services as well as school evaluation and review services. For example, the CfBT Education Trust, a U.K.-based not-for-profit education company, reviews schools in Oman under contract with the government in a role similar to that played by the Education Review Office in New Zealand (see box 4.5). In the United States, Standard and Poor's provides school evaluation services to school districts, analyzing academic, financial, and demographic indicators and trends; establishing benchmarks; and presenting findings on school performance. In addition, a number of organizations, such as www.SchoolResults.org (a public-private effort), have developed tools that enable parents to compare the performance of schools or school districts.

Private sector organizations such as the Educational Testing Service, Pearson Educational, and Kaplan in the United States, and the Center for Educational Measurement in the Philippines, provide testing and assessment services that track the education performance of schools and governments. Private school associations in the Philippines operate a voluntary accreditation scheme for private schools and higher education institutions (box 4.6), and other organizations provide information and rankings to inform students' education decisions, including provincial school report cards published annually by the Fraser Institute (www.fraserinstitute.org/reportcards/schoolperformance) and the Montreal Economic Institute (www.iedm.org/main/reportcards_en.php).

While making information freely available is an important way to improve the quality of schooling, formal independent quality assurance and monitoring mechanisms that evaluate the performance of providers and their outcomes are also needed. This would ensure independent, unbiased assessments of the performance of PPPs. Well-designed quality assurance mechanisms can provide consumers, providers, and government officials with valuable information on the performance of private schools and ensure that providers are meeting quality standards. Several mechanisms have been used around the world to assure quality in both the private and public sectors:

- Private school associations in the Philippines operate a formal accreditation system for private schools and higher education institutions.

- The De La Salle Supervised Schools Program in the Philippines provides administrative, academic, and spiritual assistance to private schools that cater predominantly to students from low- and middle-income backgrounds.

- Various public and private organizations (for example, the U.K.-based Worldwide Education Service of the CfBT Education Trust; the Education Review Office in New Zealand; and the Office for Standards in Education, Children's Services, and Skills in the UK) provide school inspection and review services.

- The Sindh Education Foundation in Pakistan operates two programs that

---

BOX 4.6   *Private school accreditation in the Philippines*

The private sector can play significant role in regulating economic activity. In the United States, many regulations are produced and enforced by independent parties and trade associations (Yilmaz 1998). Thus, there is scope for making greater use of the private sector in regulating a number of aspects of private education. The Philippines operates a private voluntary accreditation system for schools and higher education institutions. The accreditation scheme provides for four levels of accreditation that confer benefits on institutions in the form of increased operational freedom or eligibility for government assistance. The private accreditation scheme is managed and overseen by the Federation of Accrediting Agencies of the Philippines, which charges fees to cover the costs of providing this service. The federation comprises several private accreditation associations, each linked to private school associations and all of which are recognized by the government. In 2002–03, there were some 1,200 accredited programs in the Philippines.

Source: LaRocque 2002.

aim to improve the quality of education in low-fee private schools.

Foreign organizations can play an important role in helping developing countries to improve the quality of education, particularly those countries where corruption in the education sector is endemic (in the areas of testing, school licensing processes, and school reviews). For example, foreign organizations such as Cambridge International Exams and the International Baccalaureate provide independently administered and internationally recognized qualifications. International school chains such as SABIS and the Global Education Management System bring a world-class curriculum to the countries in which they operate. International organizations can also help to ensure that education standards in particular countries reach international benchmarks. For example, at the tertiary education level, the International Maritime Organization is critical in enforcing international standards in seafarer education. Governments can also require schools to be accredited by international organizations or affiliated with foreign schools as a condition of their registration and operation. This model is widely used at the tertiary education level, but foreign accreditation or affiliation is expensive for education institutions.

Public and private schools should ideally be subject to the same quality assurance system, but governments too often impose quality assurance requirements and systems on private schools that they do not apply to public schools. This restricts private providers' ability to compete. The purpose of quality assurance mechanisms should be to improve the quality of education delivered and to yield better education outcomes. Too often, much of what passes as school supervision involves compliance, red tape, and the enforcement of rules that add little to a student's education experience. Unnecessary rules and regulations foster an environment that is conducive to corruption. There are other ways to assure quality in private schools, including requiring private schools to display their quality ratings determined by independent or public quality assurance institutions.

Designing public-private partnerships

Good design, while important, is not sufficient to ensure the success of a PPP in education. It must also be effectively and efficiently implemented and governments can take several actions to improve the way in which PPPs are carried out. This section presents several broad principles and guidelines for implementing education PPPs.

Employ a transparent, competitive, and multi-stage process for selecting private partners in PPPs

A key element of effective contracting is a transparent and competitive bidding process. Bidding for service delivery contracts such as school management initiatives or private finance initiative contracts should be open to all private organizations, including both for-profit and not-for-profit providers. Contracts should be open to any local, national, and international organizations that may wish to bid to operate a public school, and the bidding process should be competitive whenever possible.

Schools whose management or construction will be contracted out should be identified well in advance, and the list should be made widely available, perhaps through an easily accessible public register. The bidding process should also be set out clearly and in advance. The education authority should send out a request for proposals to all potential bidders and should publicize its request widely to encourage as many bidders as possible. The result of the bidding process should be advertised to ensure that all market participants are made aware of the identity of the successful provider.

A transparent and competitive bidding process is likely to have positive effects in both the short and long term. In the short term, competitive bidding is most likely to yield bids that deliver value for money (that is, the lowest price for a given level of desired quality) and to minimize the potential for corruption in the awarding of the contracts. Over the longer term, a competitive process is likely to build market confidence in both the bidding process and the contracting agency, thereby encouraging the growth of the market in private education services over time.

The contracting agency should use a multi-stage process to select providers of education services, and these stages should include

- clarifying requirements, including development of contract objectives and specification of desired services and expected outcomes;
- developing a procurement strategy and hiring a procurement team;
- writing the request for proposals;
- inviting expressions of interest;
- conducting contract prequalification checks in which bids are assessed against requirements and a shortlist of bidders is selected;
- interviewing the shortlist of bidders, assessing proposals in greater depth, and negotiating contractual issues with the shortlist of bidders;
- selecting the preferred bidder and awarding the contract;
- advertising the result of the selection process;
- commencing service (International Financial Services London 2001).

Savas (2000) presents a comprehensive discussion of the steps involved in contracting for the delivery of public services. Among the issues highlighted by the author are the need for a feasibility study to assess whether it is appropriate to contract out the service; the need to foster competition in the process; the mechanics and importance of a fair bidding process (the expression of interest, the bid specifications and process, and the evaluation of the bids); and the need to monitor, evaluate, and enforce the implementation of the contract.

Split the purchaser and provider roles within the education administrative agency

PPPs function best when the education department's policy and regulatory functions are kept separate and distinct from its service delivery and compliance functions. If the same government department is responsible for both purchasing and the provision (and regulation) of education, then there is a risk that it will be biased in favor of public schools because private sector competition can threaten the viability of some struggling public schools. As Eggers (1998, 28) argues, "Splitting policy functions from service delivery creates incentives for governments to become more discriminating consumers, looking beyond government monopoly providers to a wide range of public and private providers."

In the United States, some states go further in their effort to split the purchaser and provider functions in education by allowing groups seeking to open and operate a charter school to be approved by the local school district, a university, or other body such as education contracting agencies.

Build the capacity of the contracting agency

An important factor in the successful design and implementation of PPPs is the need to ensure that the government agency responsible for these partnerships has the resources, information, and skills needed to design, develop, and manage the complex contracting processes that underlie PPP programs.

First, the contracting agency should have access to reliable and accurate financial and administrative information. Also, updated and accurate baseline information on price and outputs is essential for the contracting agency to be able to make an informed assessment of the bids submitted by organizations seeking to deliver education services. For example, to be able to assess whether the bidding process is generating value for money, the contracting agency has to have reliable information on the unit costs associated with existing or alternative providers in both the public and private sectors. The contracting agency must also have access to baseline information on the education outcomes yielded by the sector in general and by the schools to be contracted out in order to be able to specify appropriate performance benchmarks for the private sector contractors.

Second, it is vital that the contracting agency employ people with the skills needed to manage the complex task of contracting with private sector partners. The skills that are needed correspond to the wide range of functions that must be undertaken by regulators, including designing, developing, and managing payment systems; accrediting and registering schools; carrying out quality assurance functions; and running private sector incentive programs. While the move toward PPPs may seem to signal the withdrawal of governments from their role in providing education, it does not. Rather, the role of government is simply changing from being the exclusive provider of a service to being the facilitator and regulator for a range of different providers. This means that the skill set required by the public sector is also changing and now encompasses skills that are very different from the skills that used to be needed.

In particular, the shift from input controls to output-based contracting means that government agencies must develop their capacity to

- assess the various services that are provided in the education sector to determine when and under what circumstances contracting, rather than direct public provision, could be used;
- design, negotiate, implement, and monitor education service contracts;
- develop legislation that sets up a competitive and transparent contracting system;
- develop appropriate quality assurance mechanisms.

The move toward PPPs in education also requires public officials to adopt a new administrative culture. As Harding (2002) noted (in relation to the health sector but it is equally applicable to education), public officials need to stop thinking of themselves as administrators and managers of public employees and other inputs, and start thinking of themselves as contract managers with the ultimate responsibility for delivering services (but not necessarily delivering those services themselves).

The contracting authority must also have the capacity to identify fraud, track payments, and ensure that claims for payment from participating schools are legitimate and accurate. It should also ensure that it

pays schools in a timely fashion. The experience with education service contracting in the Philippines is instructive in this regard, as recent audits have discovered fraud in the form of some "ghost" schools that received funding but existed in name only. In addition, payments to schools under the scheme were often delayed several months, which discouraged many potential providers from bidding for contracts to operate schools. An effective audit procedure is a vital component of any payment or fraud monitoring system, and NGOs can often be successfully employed in such roles.

Governments that need to build their capacity to implement PPPs in education can take advantage of case studies, good practice guidelines, and lessons learned disseminated by other countries with more experience with education contracting. These come in the form of manuals, checklists, toolkits, and standardized contracts. Examples include the United Kingdom's Schools Private Finance Initiative website (www.teachernet.gov.uk), which provides guidance and standardized contracts for school infrastructure PPPs, and the National Association of Charter School Authorizers' website (www.qualitycharters.org), which provides guidance for organizations that authorize the establishment of charter schools in the United States.

In many countries, governments have chosen to set up either a dedicated, cross-sectoral unit to oversee the implementation of PPPs or specialized PPP teams within sector ministries. Establishing these units is the best way to overcome capacity weaknesses such as a lack of knowledge about contracting, a dearth of the skills required to implement PPPs, high transaction costs, and poor procurement incentives that can lead to corruption.

In most of these countries, the units have been given responsibility only for infrastructure PPPs (including schools) rather than for the entire range of PPPs. However, in principle, governments could extend the remit of these PPP units to include policy formulation and coordination, technical assistance, quality control, the standardization and dissemination of information, and the promotion and marketing of PPP initiatives. PPP units in the social sectors have the potential to play a key role in providing education authorities with technical assistance in designing and implementing contracts and in standardizing PPP processes in countries with decentralized education systems. They could also play an important role in promoting and marketing the concept of public-private partnerships and of specific PPP initiatives, which tend to be more controversial in education than in other sectors.

Establish appropriate performance measures, incentives, and sanctions for failing to perform in PPP contracts

Establishing appropriate performance measures is critical in the design of any contract. Performance measures are necessary for determining whether the service provider has met the agreed terms and conditions of the contract and are even more important when they are prerequisites for determining the compensation to be paid to the contractor. The selected performance measures must be appropriate and must reflect the outcomes required by the contracting authority because the contractor's behavior will be driven largely by what will be measured and rewarded under the terms of the contract. Performance indicators should be specified as much as possible in terms of measurable outcomes (for example, learning improvements as measured by test scores, reading levels, reduced dropout rates, and reduced teacher-student absenteeism) rather than inputs (for example, hiring additional staff or spending more on particular activities).

These performance measures must be selected with care because, if badly designed, they can produce perverse incentives and lead to undesirable outcomes. For example:

- A heavy emphasis on academic outcomes in contracts may cause contractors to ignore the development of "softer" skills such as teamwork.
- An overly rigid focus on measurable outcomes may lead to the contractor paying too little attention to desirable outcomes that are more difficult to measure, such as student self-esteem.

- A strong focus on international student assessments may give schools an incentive to refuse entry to any students who are unlikely to be strong performers academically.

This is not to argue that performance measures should not be set or that they should not be backed up by financial incentives. Performance measures and financial incentives can help align the interests of the school with those of students and the government. Appropriate incentives can also help to ensure that schools remain focused on students' needs and keep abreast of changing demands in the marketplace. The specification of requirements at an early phase can be crucial to the eventual success of the contract and needs to be carried out carefully by a multi-disciplinary team to ensure that all aspects that influence education quality are considered. Also, these targets and expectations should be realistic and achievable.

The degree to which performance indicators can be specified will vary with the nature of the contract. It will be easier to specify these measures when the services being purchased are narrow in scope and simple to measure (for example, remedial instruction and literacy programs) than when the services being purchased are broader in scope and harder to measure (for example, whole school management).

Performance indicators can be measured both qualitatively and quantitatively and can be reported at different intervals. For example, quantitative indicators such as standardized test scores, attendance rates, and dropout rates can be supplemented by qualitative methods of assessing performance, such as surveys of parents and teachers and site visits by third parties to assess progress in areas such as leadership development, the arts, and character development. Education service contracts should also include performance incentives and should make payment conditional on the contractor achieving the performance measures. There are many examples of PPPs (including private finance initiatives such as the Bogota Concession Schools program and the Punjab Education Foundation's Foundation Assisted Schools Program) that include performance measures in their contracts and that make the contractors' compensation (or continued participation in programs) conditional on their satisfactory performance.

Of course, these performance incentives and sanctions will be utterly ineffective if the education authority lacks the ability or capacity to monitor contractors' performance. This monitoring should aim both to prevent fraud and to ensure that the objectives and targets of the contract are met, especially in complex PPPs such as private finance initiatives and funding-based initiatives (for example, school management and school subsidy programs). A particular risk in PPPs that receive per student funding is the potential for unscrupulous contractors to inflate enrollment figures or to claim funds for schools that only exist on paper. Various PPP programs have adopted strategies to address this risk, including school accreditation schemes, requiring contractors to allow open access to school enrollment data, and third-party validation of enrollment figures.

Develop an effective communications strategy

Efforts to involve the private sector in education often face concerted opposition from rival political parties, labor unions, the media, the public at large, and specific interest groups. Therefore, a crucial component of any PPP in education is an effective strategic (as opposed to piecemeal or ad hoc) communication plan as this can substantially reduce political risk and be an effective way of promoting a PPP initiative. A strategic communication plan needs to be built on ongoing opinion research that assesses how various stakeholders are affected by the initiative. The results of this research will help the government determine what steps to take to build support for, promote participation in, and mitigate social opposition to, the private participation initiative.

The strategy may include featuring specific PPPs at the school level, stressing the desirable objectives and the solid experience of the private contractors. This can educate stakeholders about the potential advantages and disadvantages of PPPs, inform the general public about the academic benefits that can accrue from involving private partners in education, and promote best practices in developing and applying PPPs. The World Bank's 2004 toolkit for public communications programs on privatization is a useful resource even though PPPs do not involve outright privatization.

Introduce a framework for evaluating program outcomes

Each PPP should be accompanied by a well-designed, rigorous evaluation. Although a wide range of PPPs exists around the world, there is a lack of rigorous evidence on the impact of these programs (World Bank 2006). This is especially true for PPPs operating outside the United States and for nonvoucher programs. As noted in Patrinos (2005), the best evaluations of programs involve experiments that randomly assign benefits and include a true control group. In the absence of a random design or some form of natural experiment, it is preferable to use such rigorous techniques as propensity score matching, local average treatment effects, and regression discontinuities.

Education PPPs are highly amenable to proper impact evaluations because many of the interventions are output-driven. Having more rigorous impact evaluations is important because this would increase the amount of information available to policymakers when they make decisions about program design as well as expanding the international knowledge about the circumstances under which particular types of on education PPPs work best.

Involve international organizations in fostering PPPs

International organizations can play several roles in promoting PPPs. A key one is providing "early stage" equity and loan capital to promote investments in private education. Schools find it difficult to access investment capital with a sufficiently long time horizon. Private equity companies are generally not interested because they expect short-term returns on their investments. International lenders can raise the profile of private education as a legitimate sector for investment, and they can also work with banks to mitigate some investment risks in the sector. International organizations can also build the capacity of both banks and the education sector and help countries to create enabling regulatory frameworks for private education.

The focus of most international organization projects is on improving public sector schools and tertiary education institutions. As Sosale (2000) shows, World Bank lending for education projects totaled $4.9 billion in 1995–97, but only 11 of 70 projects (about 15 percent) included a private sector component and only about half of those were at the primary or secondary level. However, this has changed in the last decade. In 2007, 57 percent of World Bank education projects had a PPP component (Baksh, forthcoming).

In addition, the World Bank provides policy support to governments that are looking for effective ways to involve the private sector in providing education. It has also created a unit to conduct more and better quality evaluations of the impact of PPPs on education. The International Finance Corporation (IFC) also supports private education projects. It has funded operations, including one in Ghana, that provide education entrepreneurs with access to capital and has recently launched a microcredit program in Kenya, which targets private school operators and includes a technical assistance facility (box 4.7).

BOX 4.7 *Microcredit facilities for education*

Private schools in Sub-Saharan Africa have limited access to medium- and long-term investment capital. Few local banks lend to private schools, and most loans are for very short periods. Many schools also need technical assistance to build their financial, managerial, and administrative capabilities and to operate more efficiently.

The investment component will support school loans from partner banks. These loans will be used to finance the construction of facilities, the purchase of educational materials, and other capital expenditures. To be eligible for financing, schools will need to meet the partner bank's underwriting criteria. The program will focus initially on 10 countries that have high enrollment rates in private schools.

Source: IFC 2007.

Conclusions

Despite recent increases, enrollment rates remain low in several developing regions, and the quality of education lags considerably behind that in developed countries. Given market failures and equity considerations in many countries, the public sector continues to be an important player in providing education services. However, increasing access, equity, and achievement in education in developing countries will require innovative programs and initiatives from the private sector as well as public resources and leadership. One form of public-private partnership (PPP) that has been tried in education and other sectors involves the government contracting with private organizations to provide a specified service of a defined quantity and quality at an agreed price for a specific period of time. When central and local governments provide the finance for education services but contract out the actual provision of those services to the private sector, this can help to improve the quality of education and rapidly expand access to schooling, especially for under-served parts of the population.

Nevertheless, PPPs are a controversial subject. Some studies suggest that this arrangement can lead to students being segregated by income level and academic achievement, with no improvement in average academic achievement. Other studies suggest that, in large-scale voucher programs, the positive effects of competition benefit only high-achieving students and that not all parents choose their children's schools based only on academic criteria. While private participation in primary and secondary education has increased significantly over the last two decades in various forms of contracting models, there is not enough rigorous research on the effects of contracting in education to be able to draw many definite conclusions at this time.

A framework for understanding public-private partnerships in education

For education services to be provided successfully, all participants—citizens, service providers, and governments—should be held accountable. Contracting in education can improve service delivery by clearly assigning responsibilities among these actors, identifying objectives and outputs, gathering information on the performance of the partnership in order to assess its progress, and ensuring enforceability of the contracts.

Many forms of contracting are currently used in education in developing countries. Some governments buy the services involved in producing education (inputs), such as teacher training, management, curriculum design, or the use of a school facility from private organizations. Other governments contract with private organizations to manage and operate public schools (processes), including all of the activities involved in the education process. Some other governments contract with private organizations to provide education to specific students (outputs). The challenges and potential benefits of contracting for services that are inputs, processes, or outputs are very different. There are seven main forms of contracts:

- *Management services.* Weak school management is a common constraint to improving public school performance. To address it, some governments have brought in private organizations to manage public schools. Management contracts can entail the private organization managing a single school or an entire school district. Its responsibilities usually fall into four categories: financial management, staff management, long-term planning, and leadership. Nonmanagerial personnel usually remain as public sector employees.

- *Support services.* Noninstructional activities, including maintenance, student transportation, and school meals, are often very costly for public schools. Policymakers in many countries have contracted out these kinds of support services to increase cost-effectiveness and free up resources and time so that school staff can focus on the learning process. Usually, governments tender contracts that cover multiple schools so that contract management expertise can be developed in a single place and so that the contracts are large enough to attract many bidders.

- *Professional services.* Contracting out professional services such as teacher training, the provision of textbooks, curriculum design, and quality certification of schools is straightforward and usually effective. Its main advantage is that it brings private providers' expertise to bear on public education. The content and oversight of contracts are critical when buying inputs. Simple input services are relatively easy to specify in contractual terms, and the performance of the contractors can also be conveniently monitored. Also, because there are almost always many potential providers, contractors must be competitive to be awarded a contract, and the government can credibly threaten cancelation if the provider's performance is not up to par. Another advantage is that economies of scale can often be achieved because one organization can deliver these input services to multiple schools under many contracts.

- *Operational services.* In some countries, the government contracts with private organizations to operate public schools. In these operational contracts, private agencies both manage and staff the pub-

lic school. The aims of these initiatives are usually to free schools from public service constraints, give them autonomy, and to harness the interest and knowledge of parents and other community members to improve the oversight of the school. In many cases, the local community also contributes to the construction, upkeep, or improvement of school facilities.

- *Education services.* Instead of engaging a private entity to operate a public school, some governments pay for students to enroll in private schools, thus, in essence, buying outputs. By enrolling students in existing private schools, governments can quickly expand access without having to spend the money to build and equip new schools. Other governments pay for students to access specialized services in the private sector, such as alternative education not available in the public sector. When governments contract for education services, they are underwriting individual student enrollment by means of vouchers, scholarships, or per pupil subsidies, all of which make it possible to target benefits to specific students and groups.

- *Facility availability.* Governments have tried to mobilize private investment in needed capital stock in many different sectors, including education. Contracting for the provision of school facilities is appealing because it relieves governments of having to provide capital up front and all at once. Contracting for the private finance and construction of facilities allows the government to pay for these capital investments over the term of the contract instead of all at once.

- *Facility availability and education services.* Sometimes, governments contract with the same private firm not only to build the facility but also to undertake all of the activities associated with delivering education and related services. In these cases, the government simultaneously implements two forms of contract with the same operator—a contract for facility financing, development, and availability and a long-term contract for providing education services. The rationale cited most often for this form of dual contracting is to obtain necessary capital investment while giving the contractor a big incentive to organize and deliver services as efficiently as possible. The efficiency gains that the private organization can capture from both constructing and operating the schools may make up for the potentially high costs of borrowing.

International experiences of using public-private partnerships to fund existing private schools

Many governments around the world have been exploring different ways to involve the private sector in providing education, including vouchers, subsidies, capitation grants, stipends, and contracts. In addition, demand-side mechanisms such as vouchers have the advantage of promoting parental choice, school competition, and accountability. The idea is that parents choose the best school for their children on the grounds of quality, which in turn puts pressure on schools to compete to attract students and to achieve better academic results at a lower cost.

The most common type of partnership is where the government funds existing private schools, mainly to increase access to education but also to enhance quality by enabling poor students to attend better-performing private schools and to increase school competition to promote efficiency. Governments are increasingly recognizing that PPPS have a useful role to play in education and are developing institutions, funding mechanisms, and regulatory frameworks to leverage private capacity and expertise to enhance public education.

Countries lie on a continuum in the extent to which they are using PPPs. This continuum ranges from those countries in which education is provided only by the public sector to those in which it is largely publicly funded but privately provided. Countries in which the government is fully responsible for education and related services and assumes all regulatory and financing functions have no PPP environment. Countries that allow private schools to operate within a centrally determined regulatory framework but provide them with no funding from the public budget can be described as having a "nascent" PPP environment. Countries where the government subsidizes private schools can be described as having an "emerging" PPP environment. A "moderate" PPP environment is evident in those countries where the government enters into contracts with private schools that requires them (and pays them per pupil) to educate a specified number of students for a specified length of time. In countries with an "engaged" PPP environment, private organizations sign an agreement with the government to manage and operate public schools in exchange for payment from the public budget. In the strongest or "integral" PPP environment, the public sector funds private schools by providing students with vouchers that will pay for their education at whatever school they choose to attend, thus encouraging student choice and school competition (see figure 2.1 in chapter 2).

Some governments have used universal voucher programs to increase access to high-quality schooling and to make schools more diverse. Several high-income countries have school financing systems that use vouchers or similar mechanisms, including Belgium, the Czech Republic, Denmark, Ireland, the Netherlands, and Sweden. Prominent features of voucher systems include the following characteristics:

- Funding is based on expressed demand by parents.
- All private schools share the risk that without students they will have to close.
- Private schools are diverse and innovative.
- Parents and students can freely choose between public and private schools.
- Finance and provision are separate.
- All schools must comply with education standards defined by the central government.

Developing countries have begun to recognize the important role that private schools can play in increasing access and improving the quality of education through competition. Several countries subsidize private schools, mostly faith-based nonprofit organizations, either by funding school inputs (such as teachers' salaries and textbooks) or through per pupil grants. The governments of The Gambia, Mauritius, Tanzania, and Uganda have formed alliances with private schools to deliver education. Recently, as a result of the drive towards universal primary education, there has been more demand for education than the public education systems in many countries can handle. This problem, coupled with limited public funding, has resulted in a growth in the number of private low-cost schools that cater to low-income students.

Experience with PPPs across the world has shown the importance of: (i) strengthening the capacity of public education agencies to regulate, monitor, and contract with private schools; (ii) building the capacity of private providers to deliver high-quality education by giving them more access to capital and technical assistance to help them to improve their educational and management practices; and (iii) creating institutions to implement PPPs and to guarantee access to information about educational outcomes of schools.

Targeting voucher programs to underserved populations (such as girls and disadvantaged, hard to reach, and minority students) can increase equity in access to schooling and in eventual educational achievement. A program in Bangladesh that gave stipends to girls substantially increased girls' enrollment. A similar program in Pakistan helped to solve the undersupply of education services in urban areas by encouraging new private schools to open. Another way to target is to use funding formulas that favor students from lower-income families. For instance, in South Africa, the government categorizes public and private schools on the basis of their relative poverty level and provides them with subsidies based on the level of tuition and other fees that they require their students to pay. As a result, the poorest schools receive the highest subsidies.

Contracts to provide education services are another kind of PPP in which the public sector contracts with private providers to educate a specific number of students in exchange for a per pupil payment. These contracts differ from voucher-like programs in that they introduce a risk-sharing element. The public and private sectors face the same risk of financial loss for noncompliance and share the same incentives to improve their performance.

Governments can contract with NGOs to provide professional and support services to public and private schools that cater to low-income students. For example, in some situations, the capacity of the public sector to deliver high-quality education is compromised by a lack of knowledge about effective pedagogical practices. PPPs enable governments to introduce into public schools education methods that have proven to be effective in private schools by contracting with private agencies to provide teacher training, curriculum design, textbooks, and supplemental services. In Colombia, the government contracts with the Escuela Nueva Foundation to train rural schoolteachers, distribute textbooks, update curricula, and provide technical assistance to rural schools.

Governments can also contract with private organizations to take over the operation of entire schools, including teaching, management, finance and staffing, support services, and building maintenance. Schools that are publicly funded but privately managed have the potential to improve quality and increase efficiency because they have more autonomy than traditional public schools, which means that they are subject to fewer constraints such as bureaucratic requirements and pressure from teachers' unions. In addition, in schools that are publicly funded but privately managed, decisions about school management are made at a level that is closer to the beneficiary than in other schools. When governments make such operation contracts with private organizations, they are leveraging not only the organization's expertise, but also its innovative instructional and management practices. Publicly funded private schools can transform the education system from the outset, simply by providing a wider range of schooling alternatives. Moreover, because they must offer free education, they provide additional places for students who are traditionally underserved.

The United States has a highly decentralized education system and an active capital market that invests in for-profit education management organizations and institutions that channel funds to education businesses. Consequently, the United States is the country with the most experience with contracting for the private operation of public schools. There are two types of private management of schools in the United States—education management organizations and charter schools. Other countries are following suit. The government of Qatar introduced the independent school program in 2004 as part of an overarching decentralization reform; the management of all public schools will be transferred to independent operators by 2011 in order to promote accountability and improve academic performance. Latin America has two examples of privately managed public schools. The first one is Venezuela's Fe y Alegría Network, which provides free education to poor communities in underserved areas and receives funding from the government through an agreement between the Ministry of Education and the Venezuelan Association of Catholic Education. Fe y Alegría schools account for 8 percent of total enrollments in Venezuela. In Colombia, the concession model was created in 1999 to provide high-quality education to low-income students. Concession school operators are private schools or universities that have excellent academic performance records.

Contracting out school operations can replicate and scale up successful practices to bring them within reach of more students. The World Bank's *World Development Report 2004* identifies a lack of systematic learning from innovation and insufficient replication of successful practices as problems at the basic education level. Two additional ways to give schools an incentive to improve their outputs are to allow the most competent operators to manage more schools and to standardize good practices based on either on local research or proven examples of success on the ground.

Publicly funded private schools lead to innovation and experimentation because they have autonomy over the selection and implementation of their educational strategies. Also, contracts for operational service attract a wide range of different kinds of private providers, which means that the supply of education becomes more diversified. Colombia, Qatar, and the United States have explicitly created incentives to attract high-performing or specialized education organizations to drive up the overall quality of the education provided in those countries. In Colombia, bidders to run concession schools had to show that they already operated education institutions that had scored above the average on national examinations. Qatar allowed international operators to bid to run schools and allowed providers to make a reasonable profit as an incentive to attract bidders.

In many of the PPP models, decision-making power over school management is transferred to the school itself, which makes the provider much more immediately accountable to the user of the service (parents, students, and local communities) and which tends to lead swiftly to increased efficiencies in inputs and improvements in service. Although privately operated public schools spend less money per pupil than public schools do, they are more successful in raising their students' academic achievement. One reason for this is that they have more autonomy than public schools to make decisions about pedagogical methods and the management of their financial and human resources. Although the concept of a charter school requires open enrollment and free education, these schools are allowed to tailor their curricula to target specific populations, such as likely dropouts or students with a particular academic interest.

The United Kingdom's private finance initiative model allows private consortiums and public authorities to become partners with the government in the construction and maintenance of education facilities. This kind of initiative has been accompanied by a substantial growth in the global pool of capital available for investment in infrastructure. Infrastructure funds manage an estimated $133 billion, 77 percent of which was raised between 2006 and 2007 (Palter, Walder, and Westlake 2008). This model has now spread from the United Kingdom to several European countries as well as Australia, Canada, and Egypt.

What do we know about public-private partnerships in education?

Increasing the private sector's role in education through PPPs can have several benefits over traditional public delivery of education, including greater efficiency, increased choice, and wider access to government services, particularly for people who are poorly served by traditional schools. Increased private involvement in education, through contracting or vouchers, may also increase the expertise and capacity of the education sector and has the advantage of avoiding the operating restrictions faced by traditional public schools, such as inflexible salary scales and work rules.

The main goals that governments hope to achieve by contracting with the private sector in education are to increase enrollment, improve educational outcomes (such as standardized tests scores and dropout rates), and widen access to education for low-income families. They also hope to reduce the costs of providing education while increasing its cost-effectiveness.

This book has assessed the strengths of four types of contracts—vouchers, subsidies, private management, and private finance initiatives—in the context of four main objectives—increasing enrollment, improving education outcomes, reducing inequality, and reducing costs. In terms of enrollment, vouchers and subsidies can deliver very strong results, as long as the private supply is adequate. However, these contracts may cause students to desert public schools for better-performing private schools. Private management and private finance initiatives presumably require large initial capital investment in the construction of schools, which in turn may limit their ability to produce substantial changes in enrollments. Vouchers, subsidies, and private contracts can have strong links with education outcomes. In contrast, private finance initiatives' power to influence education outcomes is small.

The main challenge involved in evaluating contracting programs is the problem of endogeneity, which typically arises because of self-selection. The challenge is to build the right comparison group, whose data can be compared with those involved in the contracts to judge the program's effectiveness. This challenge exists in the case of all impact evaluations of any kind, but in education it is exacerbated by the fact that self-selection comes from two sources—schools and students. For instance, in subsidy programs, schools first decide whether to apply for the subsidy and then students decide which school to attend, based partly on whether the school receives a subsidy or not. There are six empirical strategies that can be used to overcome endogeneity—randomization, regression discontinuity analysis, instrumental variables, Heckman correction models, difference in difference estimators, and propensity score-matching (see appendix B).

Although only very few empirical studies of the impact of PPPs exist, it is possible to draw some useful lessons about the feasibility of certain contracts. It seems that the private management of public schools has had a positive impact on student test scores. Less is known, however, about what exactly it is about charter and concession schools that make them perform better than other schools.

Most studies have shown that the private management of public schools is effective in a range of respects. The body of evaluation evidence on charter schools in the United States has grown substantially in recent years. This research has found that, initially, students in charter schools seem to score lower than their peers in public schools on standardized tests, but after a period of time (usually three years), their scores increase to levels similar to those of their public school peers. Evidence from randomized interventions from Chicago has shown that the positive effects of a charter school education on test scores are concentrated in the early grades. Studies of Colombia and Venezuela similarly concluded that privately managed schools tend to yield higher test scores than public institutions for students at the end of their basic education. These two studies used propensity score matching estimators with only limited data, and, therefore, their results should only be used with care.

Vouchers are associated with much controversy. Several countries allow parents to choose to send their children to any school, provide public funding for private and religious schools, and allocate resources to schools based on their enrollment rates—in short, voucher-like systems. Some of these systems are more than 100 years old, such as those in Denmark and the Netherlands, while others are more recent, such as those in Chile and Sweden. Colombia's targeted program has been the subject of extensive analysis because of its randomized design. Colombia's program is well targeted, effective, and efficient. It provided quality education to more than 125,000 students at a lower cost than public schools did, and much of this positive effect has been shown to be a result of competition. On the other hand, the evaluation evidence of the voucher reform of 1981 in Chile is mixed. While some studies found the reform to have had positive effects, others have challenged these findings as having problems of selection bias and a lack of adequate instruments. Furthermore, for many years following the voucher reform, overall school quality in Chile did not improve. Things have been changing more recently, as there have been rapid increases in test scores. In general, in most universal voucher programs in Europe, the availability of school choice has led to a more competitive schools market, and in most cases this competition has led to better outcomes overall, as would be predicted by theory. Nevertheless, there is much to learn about school choice and vouchers.

Two types of PPPs on which much more research effort is needed are subsidies (public funds given to private schools) and private finance initiatives (long-term government contracts with private partners to provide school infrastructure). However, neither the lack of evidence in one area nor the positive results in another are reasons to ignore PPPs or to embark on a large-scale expansion. Such programs should be piloted and rigorously evaluated in different settings, and this study provides guidance on how to conduct better evaluations in these important areas.

The empirical literature on vouchers is large and technically strong. The evidence on the other three types of contracts—subsidies, private management, and private finance initiatives—is less abundant, with the evidence on the impact of private management mainly consisting of the charter school literature in the United States. Therefore, more research on the relationship between PPPs and education outcomes is urgently needed. Future evaluations of PPP models need to be rigorously designed from the outset.

Improving education policy and regulatory frameworks

Some policy changes can provide an enabling policy and regulatory frameworks for private schools in developing countries. Such a framework would create the conditions under which private schools can operate effectively and efficiently, while ensuring that education is still of high quality.

Provide a sound basis for the private school sector. In many countries, the current climate in the education sector is hostile to private providers of education, particularly those that are for-profit. Some governments do not allow any for-profit schools to be opened at all, while others try to limit or tax any surpluses that they may make. However, once governments recognize the benefits that private education can yield to the sector as a whole, they can start by adopting a policy that clearly welcomes private providers and encourages them to establish new schools or universities. Ideally, this policy statement would define the place of private providers in the national long-term education strategy to give potential investors and partners the confidence to invest.

Consider allowing private schools to set their own tuition and other fees. Many countries and jurisdictions, including Ghana, India, the Sindh province of Pakistan, the Philippines, and Vietnam, limit the tuition and fees that private schools can charge, require that they consult the governments about any increases, or regulate the distribution of tuition fees. These restrictions do not encourage private providers to get involved in increasing the supply of education. If, instead, governments allowed private schools to set their own fees, this would give private providers an incentive to invest in the education sector.

Consider allowing both not-for-profit and for-profit schools to operate. Several governments restrict the extent to which for-profit providers can operate in the education sector or limit the funding for not-for-profit private schools. However, this bias against for-profit provision is not universal. Private for-profit schools are growing in many countries. While private schools are often seen as catering solely to the wealthy, the reality is that for-profit schools provide a significant number of places to the poor. Private for-profit schools come in a variety of forms, including single owner-operated schools, chains that operate a large number of schools, and education management organizations, such as Edison Schools. For-profit schools serve the full range of communities, including elite families, middle-income families, and the poor.

Promote and facilitate foreign direct investment in education. Foreign direct investment in education is small but growing in developed countries, developing economies, and transition economies. In 2005, foreign direct investment in education globally was nearly $3.5 billion, up from just $86 million in 1990 and $401 million in 2002, and most of this investment has been in developed countries. However, foreign direct investment in education remains smaller than in other sectors of the economy. In 2007, it accounted for less than 0.1 percent of foreign direct investment in the service sector. Therefore, there is scope for governments of developing countries to promote and facilitate foreign direct investment in their education systems.

Establish clear and objective establishment criteria and streamline processes for registering private schools. Many countries limit the scope for new providers to enter the education marketplace. Many of these regulations are aimed at protecting consumers, which is a laudable objective. Establishing minimum standards can help to ensure the quality and safety of private sector provision while still protecting consumers from unscrupulous operators. However, poorly designed registration criteria for private

schools often have the opposite impact of what is intended. Rather than increasing access, improving quality, and making schools safer, overly restrictive registration criteria, long and convoluted school registration processes, and onerous mandatory regulations can deter potential providers or increase their costs so much that the schools become unaffordable. Alternatively, such regulation may push schools to operate outside the law as unregistered or clandestine providers, meaning that the government would have fewer ways to protect consumers. This can impose costs on consumers, and invariably these costs will fall disproportionately on the poor, who have fewer education options. In particular, governments can ensure that school registration criteria are

- realistic and achievable, while meeting policy goals efficiently and effectively;
- objective and measurable, to minimize discretion and limit scope for corruption;
- transparent and available to prospective private school entrants;
- output-focused to allow for flexible and diverse delivery approaches;
- applied consistently across various levels of government.

Give subsidies to the private school sector. In addition to providing general investment incentives, governments can encourage private investment in education by offering monetary or in-kind subsidies to private schools. These subsidies can be given up front, for example, as free or discounted land, establishment grants, or education infrastructure. Land can be especially important in urban areas where it is expensive. Governments can also encourage private investment by facilitating work visas for foreign teachers, management, and technical staff. It is important to ensure that private schools have sustainable funding to underwrite their effective operation and to minimize corruption in the delivery of services. Broadly speaking, governments should preside over school funding systems that are integrated, neutral, responsive to the changing needs of schools, and targeted to low-income families. Ideally, the funding system should have the following characteristics:

- Public and private schools should be funded within the same system.
- Demand-side financing techniques should be used where necessary.
- Funding for schools should be targeted to factors that pose barriers.
- The criteria for receiving funding need to be transparent, publicly available, and easily understood.

Ensure that PPP contracts are flexible enough for private providers. The key to implementing successful PPPs is ensuring that the private partners are given considerable flexibility in terms of how they deliver the service for which they are being contracted. The government should spell out its required outputs and performance standards and set penalties for failing to achieve them and rewards for achieving them, but thereafter, they should leave providers to decide for themselves how best to deliver the required outputs to the specified standard. Providers must have as much management freedom as possible, especially in staffing and employment and budget allocations as well as over the curriculum.

Improve information flows and establish an effective quality assurance system. A key weakness in many countries is the lack of available information on the private education market. This is especially important given the growth of private education in many countries and the wide variations in price and quality. Many countries have only limited information on the fees that they charge, the programs that they offer, and the qualifications of their staff. Even the regulatory authorities have little information on either the size or nature of the private school and tertiary education sectors. Some countries publish exam scores on a school-by-school basis (for example, the Philippines and Uganda), while others have found innovative ways to provide consumers with information on the performance of schools and tertiary education institutions. Well-informed consumers and regulators are an important component of any regulatory framework for education. One way to ensure that consumers are kept informed is

for governments to put stringent requirements on education providers to disclose information about their operations. This could be done by

- requiring schools to disclose information to regulators and the general public,
- introducing a system for collecting and disseminating information from schools on a number of specific indicators,
- introducing school reviews to collect information, and
- creating independent review and accrediting agencies.

Implementing education public-private partnerships in developed and developing countries

Good design, while important, is not sufficient to ensure the success of a PPP in education. It must also be effectively and efficiently implemented. Weak implementation of PPPs can expose governments to substantial financial and policy risks, but governments can take several actions to improve the way in which PPPs are implemented.

Employ a transparent, competitive, and multi-stage process for selecting private partners in PPPs. A key element of effective contracting is a transparent and competitive bidding process. Bidding for service delivery contracts such as school management initiatives or private finance initiative contracts should be open to all private organizations, including for-profit and not-for-profit providers. Contracts should be open to any local, national, and international organizations that may wish to bid for the opportunity to operate a public school. The contracting agency should select providers by means of a multi-stage process, and these stages should consist of

- clarifying requirements, including objectives, services, and outcomes;
- developing a procurement strategy and identifying a technically strong procurement team;
- writing the request for proposals;
- inviting expressions of interest;
- conducting contract prequalification checks;

- interviewing bidders, assessing proposals, and negotiating with a shortlist of bidders;
- selecting the preferred bidder and awarding the contract;
- advertising the result of the selection process;
- commencing the service.

Split the purchaser and provider roles within the education administrative agency. PPPs function better when the education department separates its purchaser role from its provider role. In this situation, the ministry's policy and regulatory functions are kept separate and distinct from its service delivery and compliance functions. If the same government department is responsible for both purchasing and provision (and regulation) of education, there is a risk that it will be biased in favor of public schools because private sector competition can threaten the viability of some public schools.

Build the capacity of the contracting agency. The key to successfully designing and implementing PPPs is to ensure that the government agency responsible for PPPs has the resources, information, and skills needed to design, develop, and manage the complex contracting processes that underlie PPP programs. In particular, the recent shift away from input controls to output-based contracting means that government agencies must develop their capacity to

- assess services to determine when contracting is appropriate;
- design, negotiate, implement, and monitor education service contracts;
- develop legislation that supports a competitive and transparent system;
- develop appropriate quality assurance mechanisms.

Establish appropriate performance measures and include performance incentives and sanctions for failing to perform in PPP contracts. Establishing appropriate performance measures is critical in the design of all contracts. Performance measures are necessary for determining whether the service provider has met the agreed terms and conditions of the contract. Performance measures are even more important when they are prerequisites in the contract to the provider's compensation. The performance measures and standards in each case must be carefully designed because they can introduce perverse incentives and lead to undesirable outcomes. For example, it is usually desirable to bear in mind the following issues:

- A heavy emphasis on test scores may crowd out focus on other skills.
- Setting measurable outcomes may lead providers to pay too little attention to achieving other desirable outcomes.
- High scores in external tests may provide schools with an incentive to select only strong students.

Develop an effective communications strategy. Efforts to involve the private sector in education often face concerted opposition from rival political parties, labor unions, the media, the public at large, and specific interest groups. Therefore, a crucial component of any PPP in education is an effective, strategic (as opposed to piecemeal or ad hoc) communications strategy, as this can substantially reduce political risk and be an effective way of promoting a PPP initiative.

Introduce a framework for evaluating program outcomes. PPPs should be accompanied by a well-designed, rigorous evaluation. Although a wide range of PPPs exists around the world, there is a lack of rigorous evidence on the impact of these partnerships on academic outcomes and other education indicators. This is especially true for PPPs outside the United States and for nonvoucher programs.

Recommendations

Where appropriate, PPPs can increase access and improve quality in education by giving students choices and by putting competitive pressures on schools. Public funding of private schools is justified because disadvantaged students will benefit from the opportunity to enroll in schools appropriate for their needs. Nevertheless, ensuring academic quality in this kind of education system is a persistent challenge. Experience with PPPs in various countries yields the following recommendations:

- *Include output specifications that define performance standards and facilitate the measurement and tracking of quality and school efficiency.* Performance indicators can be quantitative, such as standardized tests or enrollment figures, or qualitative, such as school and parent surveys or school inspections. It is particularly important to include quality indicators that will encourage improvements in the performance of private schools and, equally important, to reinforce them with appropriate supervision.

- *Define operating requirements and performance standards that private schools and operators should follow.* Private schools should meet eligibility criteria to receive public funding (such as infrastructure and staff requirements), follow national curricula, and meet performance benchmarks.

- *Reward innovation and quality improvements.* One way to reward schools is to provide monetary awards for good performance. Conversely, sanctions for poor performance should include the revoking of any subsidies.

- *Help private schools to deliver high-quality education and accompany voucher programs with capacity-building interventions.* Some private schools lack the capacity to improve the quality of the education that they provide because their teachers lack qualifications, the schools lack the resources to buy materials and textbooks, and school management is not aware of the most effective teaching techniques and management processes. Some ways to help build this kind of capacity in private schools include increasing their access to capital and preferential loans to improve infrastructure and other critical inputs; and providing technical assistance and quality certification to enhance financial management, instructional delivery, and school leadership.

- *Establish a specialized group of authorities to manage PPP programs and the flow of funds from the government to private schools, and to enforce qualifying criteria and regulations.*

The role of the World Bank Group

International organizations can be vital in promoting high-quality private education in several ways. They can provide "early stage" equity and loan capital to finance investments in the private education sector. Private schools sometimes find it difficult to access short-term (five to seven years) investment capital because private equity is generally not interested in such a short time horizon. International lenders can help to increase the attractiveness of the private education sector as an investment target. They can also work with private sector banks to mitigate some of their investment risks. Also, they can increase the capacity of both private banks and the education sector and help countries to create regulatory frameworks that enable the development of private education in developing countries.

The main focus of most education projects supported by international organizations is on improving public sector schools and tertiary education institutions. However, the International Finance Corporation (IFC) also provides financial and technical support to private education projects, including operations that provide education entrepreneurs in Ghana with access to capital, and it has recently launched a microcredit program in Kenya, which targets private school providers and includes a technical assistance facility component.

	Country	Program	Program Description	Objective	Partners
			Educational Services		
1	Argentina	Public funding for private schools	Private school coverage at the primary and secondary level was approximately 26.4% in 2005. Local education authorities provide public resources to support teacher salaries, totally or partially, in 65% of private schools. In 2005, the total amount of public resources transferred to private schools represented 13% of local education budgets, which is equivalent to 0.47% of GDP. The Law of Education Finance does not establish a concrete formula for transferring public resources to private schools.	Increase access	Local education authorities, public schools
2	Australia	Public funding for independent schools	Independent schools receive both recurrent and capital funding, with the former being the larger of the two components. Recurrent funding is provided both in the form of general per-student grants and specific funding aimed at targeted groups of students. Payments to individual schools are based on a sliding scale that depends on a school's socioeconomic status. In 2007, enrollments in nongovernment schools represented over 33% of total enrollments.	Increase access and improve quality	Private, religious, and public schools, government of Australia
3	Bangladesh	Female Secondary School Assistance Project	Scholarships cover the direct cost of girls' secondary education. Once girls have satisfied a set of requirements, the corresponding schools are paid the entire tuition amount. Additionally, girls receive a stipend expected to cover 50% of school fees. Other components of the project include curriculum reform, instructional materials development, teacher training, the improvement of school infrastructure, and institutional capacity building.	Increase access	Government of Bangladesh, Asian Development Bank, the World Bank, public and private schools
4	Bangladesh	Subsidies	The government subsidizes at least 9 teachers at 90% of the government base teachers' salaries at community-managed, not-for-profit, nongovernment schools. Government subsidizes increases in enrollment by paying for additional teachers as long as the school meets the state criteria. Subsidies work like a quasi-voucher because they are tied to increased enrollment.	Increase access	Nongovernment schools, government of Bangladesh
5	Belgium	Voucher scheme	The vast majority of approved private schools receive grants from the government on the same basis as public authority schools. Staff salaries are paid directly by the government and funding is provided for other operating expenses. Assistance for the development of capital infrastructure is provided via grants, loan guarantees, and favorable interest rates. Grant-aided schools must meet minimum academic and operating standards but have the freedom to choose their educational plan. In 2004, more than 50% of enrollments at the basic and secondary levels were private. Most private schools have a religious association.	Increase access and improve quality	Public, private schools, and the state
6	Canada (Alberta)	Public funding for nongovernment schools	Accredited independent schools receive basic grants equal to 35% of public school costs. Subsidized schools must comply with operating requirements, use the Alberta Program of Studies, and follow the same accountability requirements as public schools. However, they have the freedom to establish tuition fees and admission policies.	Increase access and improve quality	Provincial government of Alberta, independent schools

continued

	Country	Program	Program Description	Objective	Partners
			Educational Services		
7	Chile	Voucher scheme	This voucher scheme involves the government paying a monthly fixed fee to subsidized private schools according to their enrollment numbers. There is price discrimination among private subsidized schools depending on their location and level of education. Families have no restrictions on school selection, but private subsidized schools are not compelled to accept any student. Subsidized schools must meet minimum requirements but enjoy management flexibility. Vouchers are paid directly to private schools. In addition, the government gives nonportable subsidies to public schools in low-income areas.	Increase access, improve quality, and support the decentralization of education	Central government, subsidized private schools, municipalities
8	Colombia	Plan de Ampliacion de la Cobertura de la Educacion Secundaria	Vouchers are made available to students from low-income families who had been attending public schools but who had been accepted into a private school. Vouchers were renewable subject to satisfactory academic performance.	Increase access to secondary schooling for children from poor families	Secretaries of Education at the departmental and municipal level and private schools
9	Colombia	Contract schools	Local governments contract private schools to deliver public education services for a determined number of students in an academic year. The private contractors assume all or some of the costs involved in educating a student and the government reimburses them on a per-pupil basis in accordance with the pre-agreed contract. In 2004, 11.2% of the students in eight cities in Colombia were enrolled in contract schools. Secretaries of Education establish the number of places needed for public school students, develop a pool of bidders for the selection of education service providers, and process contracts. A list of eligible students is presented to each private school selected. Only in one city, Cali, are parents allowed to select their children's school.	Increase access to quality education services for low-income students	Territorial entities, private schools, Ministry of Education, Secretaries of Education
10	Côte d'Ivoire	Contracts for education services	The government gives a payment to lower and upper secondary private schools for each public student that they enroll. Schools must be "chartered" to take on additional students, and placement depends in part on the educational performance of the school. Subsidies vary with school location and are loosely tied to the number of students enrolled. The number of students in the private school sponsorship program was 223,000 in 2001 (an increase from 116,000 in 1993).	Increase supply of education to meet student demand	Government of Côte d'Ivoire, private schools
11	Czech Republic	Voucher scheme	All schools, public and private, receive public funding based on the number of students enrolled. The funding consists of (1) base funding equal to 50% of state school funding, and (2) supplementary funding based on quality, assessed on the basis of explicit criteria.	Increase access and improve quality	Ministry of Education, nonstate schools
12	Denmark	Voucher scheme	Private schools, some of them organized by parents, receive grants from the central government corresponding to approximately 80% of their total expenditures. Schools must meet centrally determined standards, and teachers must possess the required qualifications. The grants take into account property-related and operating costs and vary across schools depending on their size, the age distribution of their students, and the seniority of their teachers.	Increase access and improve quality	Government of Denmark, private schools, parent boards
13	Gambia, The	Scholarships	The government funds full scholarships that cover the costs of tuition, books, and examination fees to one-third of girls in upper basic and secondary private schools with low enrollment in the most deprived regions. They also cover tuition and examination fees for 10% of girls who excel in science, math, and technology at the upper basic and secondary school level in less deprived regions.	Increase access, retention rates, and girls' enrollment rates	Private schools, Boards of Governors, and the government of The Gambia

	Country	Program	Program Description	Objective	Partners
			Educational Services		
14	Guatemala	Scholarships/ Eduque a la Nina	This program gave vouchers to girls from low-income communities to induce them to enroll in the first, second, and third grades. It was implemented in 12 rural communities and involved approximately 800 girls over 2 years. Target communities were chosen because they had the largest differentials between male and female school attendance and graduation rates. The voucher was renewed provided the girl was promoted to the next grade.	Increase access and retention rates	Public schools, parent committees, school teachers, Asociacion Eduquemos a la Nina
15	Haiti	Haiti Education For All Adaptable Program Grant	To increase access, the project will fund per student subsidies disbursed to school management committees of accredited nonpublic schools to subsidize the tuition fees and educational materials for out-of-school children. The project will also train more new teachers and contract qualified NGOs and school inspectors to strengthen the capacity of school management committees. To improve quality, the project will pilot student-centered learning programs adapted for multi-grade classrooms, support student health and nutrition programs, and strengthen private schools' capacity to deliver early indicators (grade 2) of learning outcomes, particularly basic literacy.	Increase access, improve quality, and reduce inequity	Nonpublic primary schools, Department of Administrative Affairs, school management committees, the National Education Partnership Office, the National School Feeding Program, the Department of Private Education, the Fast Track Initiative, the World Bank
16	Hungary	Voucher scheme	The guiding principles of the Hungarian system are high levels of local control, school self-management, and acceptance of school competition. Private institutions are entitled to receive per-pupil grants from municipalities. Funding for private schools is formula-based and dependent on the number of students enrolled.	Improve quality, increase efficiency, and support decentralization	Private schools, autonomous local governments
17	India	System of government grant-in-aid to privately managed schools	Grants to aided schools account for a substantial proportion of the education budget. Any recognized private school can apply for government grant-in-aid, and once granted aided status, it receives block grants in the form of the payment of all teacher salaries. Teachers are paid out of school revenues and are accountable to fee-paying parents and school managers. Teachers are managed at the school level. There is a high inter-state variation in grant-in-state aid.	Increase access	Private schools, central government
18	Italy	Voucher scheme	In 9 (of 20) regions, the government subsidizes tuition fees at private primary and secondary schools. There are (1) income-targeted vouchers that offer partial reimbursement of private school tuition, and (2) voucher programs that provide a fixed payment, conditional on school performance and family income. Schools receiving vouchers must be legally recognized by the government.	Improve quality and increase choice	National and regional governments, private schools
19	Korea, Republic of	Subsidies	Under the "leveling policy for secondary education," elementary school graduates are randomly assigned to either public or private middle schools in their district of residence. Private schools are required to meet government requirements and are not allowed to charge tuition fees. As a result, 95% of private school costs are subsidized by government, including teachers and operations.	Improve quality and reduce inequity in the school environment	Central government, private secondary schools
20	Mauritius	Subsidies	Most private schools in Mauritius are funded by the government and are non-fee-paying (some have a religious orientation). The government pays the wages of the staff of private schools and their running expenses based on a grant formula. Other indirect costs are met by students and their families (such as books, transport, and uniforms). In 2005, 66% of students in the secondary mainstream and 58% of those in prevocational education were enrolled in private schools. The program is supplemented by incentive grants such as a loan scheme for private schools with preferential interest rates to upgrade their infrastructure facilities.	Increase access and improve quality	The Mauritius Educational Development Company, the Development Bank of Mauritius, the Private Secondary Schools Authority, private schools

continued

	Country	Program	Program Description	Objective	Partners
			Educational Services		
21	Netherlands	Voucher scheme	The government funds public and private schools on an equal footing. Institutions are given considerable freedom to decide how to allocate their resources, although they must meet the government's performance requirements. School choice is promoted in order to increase competition between schools, and most students attend private schools (by 2004, 69% and 83% of enrollments at the primary and secondary level).	Increase access and improve quality	The Dutch government, private schools
22	New Zealand	Targeted Individual Entitlement	The Targeted Individual Entitlement program sought to assist children from low-income families to attend private schools, to give more choice to parents with limited options, and to increase educational attainment among low-income families. Low-income students received a subsidy (110% of the average cost of education at a state school) to attend private schools. This was a pilot program that was abolished in 2000.	Increase access and improve quality	Participating schools, the government of New Zealand
23	New Zealand	Public subsidies for independent schools	Independent schools receive subsidies of about 25% to 35% of the average per pupil cost in public schools. Subsidies are enrollment-based and vary by grade level. Schools must be registered. Subsidized schools can be for-profit, they do not have to use the national teacher's contract, and are not required to teach the national curriculum.	Increase access and improve quality	Independent schools, the government of New Zealand
24	New Zealand	Alternative education/per-pupil funding	The programs seeks to provide alternative education programs to students alienated from the education system and to prepare students to return to mainstream secondary education or move onto tertiary education once they reach 16 years of age. The program contracts out the delivery of education in nonformal settings to not-for-profit, community-based organizations or for-profit educational providers.	Increase access and retention rates	Single private schools, consortiums of private schools, not-for-profit community-based organizations, for-profit educational providers, the government
25	New Zealand	Integrated Schools	Former private schools, mainly owned by private organizations, have been integrated into the public system and receive recurrent funding equivalent to that received by public schools. Integrated schools are subject to state regulations and are not allowed to charge tuition but are allowed to charge fees to cover infrastructure expenditures. Integrated schools represented 11% of enrollments in New Zealand in 2007.	Increase access	Integrated schools and the government of New Zealand
26	Pakistan (Balochistan)	Urban Girls Fellowship	In this pilot program launched in 1995, the government paid a declining subsidy to private schools over a three-year period to enroll girls from low-income families, in addition to a tuition fee per girl per year. The subsidy was paid directly to the school and was limited to 100 girls.	Increase girls' enrollment in schools	Private schools, the Government of Balochistan, parent education committees
27	Pakistan (Balochistan)	Basic Education Support Project	Program that supports the establishment of new private schools by providing per-student subsidies to Private School Implementation Partners (PIPs) for up to four year. Schools are able to charge top up fees of up to PRs300 per month. Additionally, PIPs receive per-student subsidies for facilities and material costs. New schools will participate in the program if they have over 50 students and there is no public school in a radius of 20 kilometers.	Increase access to low-fee high-quality private education	Private schools, the World Bank, rural community schools, the Government of Balochistan
28	Pakistan (Punjab)	Financial Assistance per Child Enrolled Basis Program (FAS)	The Punjab Education Foundation pays a subsidy to participating private schools on a per pupil basis. The schools cannot charge fees on top of the per-student subsidy paid. Participating schools must meet eligibility criteria (in terms of enrollment, student composition, physical infrastructure, geographical location, the capacity to deliver quality education, and management) and register with the district government. Subsidies are paid directly to the school. The Punjab Education Foundation provides professional development support for the FAS schools.	Improve quality and increase productivity	Private eligible schools, Punjab Education Foundation

	Country	Program	Program Description	Objective	Partners
			Educational Services		
29	Pakistan (Punjab)	Pilot Education Voucher Scheme	The Pilot Education Voucher Scheme will give education vouchers to children from urban slums in Lahore. Its design will include strategies to support school improvement and quality education. The vouchers will be nontradable.	Improve quality of education and encourage girls' enrollment in schools	Punjab Education Foundation, eligible schools
30	Philippines	Educational Service Contracting (ESC)	The government contracts with private high schools to enroll students in areas where there is a shortage of places in public schools. Assistance is given only to students at institutions that charge low fees and serve low-income families. The program also includes a certification aspect. In 2008–09, around 476,776 students were subsidized under the ESC program.	Increase access and improve quality	Certified private schools, Fund for Assistance to Private Education, and the Department of Education
31	Qatar	Voucher scheme	The voucher system allows parents to choose among independent, private accredited, and international schools. The schools remain autonomous and are held accountable for student learning. The variety of schooling options will, over time, give parents a growing range of different kinds of schools to choose from when selecting the best school for their children.	Improve quality and increase educational choices to raise academic achievement	The Supreme Education Council, independent or accredited voucher schools
32	Senegal	Scholarships	Communaute Urbaine de Dakar is an agglomeration of five municipalities that offers scholarships to students studying in both private and public schools inside or outside of Senegal.	Increase access and improve quality	Municipalities, private schools (national or international)
33	South Africa	Subsidies	State funding to public and private schools is organized on a quintile system, in which schools are divided into five categories according to the poverty levels that prevail in the areas that they serve. Schools in the lowest two quintiles receive full funding from the government. Private schools requesting funding must provide evidence of sound management and financial records and allow unannounced inspections by the provincial education department.	Increase access and reduce inequity	Public and private providers of education, provincial education departments
34	Sweden	Voucher scheme	Municipalities give capitation grants to private and public schools on an equal footing. They have more authority over their own (public) schools than over private schools but have full financial responsibility for the whole school system. Independent schools often have a particular academic focus such as religion, art, sports, or music. Schools must be approved by the National Agency for Education and meet certain regulatory requirements in order to be eligible for government funding.	Increase access and improve quality	The National Agency for Education, municipalities, private primary and secondary schools
35	Thailand	Subsidies	The government of Thailand provides monthly subsidies to private schools on a cost-per-student basis. This is a major source of income for most schools. Private schools are allowed to charge fees similar to tuition fees to improve the quality of education; additional fees are allowed for meals, transportation, health inspection, and other extras. Private schools providing basic education can qualify for state-subsidized loans to build new school buildings or to renovate old ones. The government also has a revolving fund for private schools, which offers 4 % interest loans with a repayment period of 10–15 years to schools that can offer collateral.	Increase access and improve quality	Private and public schools, the central government, foundations, and parents' associations
36	Uganda	Universal Secondary Education Program	The government of Uganda subsidizes 430 private secondary schools serving approximately 56,000 students (as of 2008) in order to attain universal secondary education. The Ministry of Education chooses the participating schools and a memorandum of understanding is signed with individual private schools to ensure that they comply with the policy's implementation guidelines.	Increase access	Private secondary schools, the Ministry of Education and Sports in Uganda

continued

	Country	Program	Program Description	Objective	Partners
			Educational Services		
37	United Kingdom	Assisted Places Scheme	The Assisted Places Scheme was introduced in 1980 and provided financial support for poor students with high academic achievement to attend private schools. The program served about 30,000 students in 1993/94 and was abolished in 1997. Additionally, a demand-driven funding system for public schools was introduced in 1998. Seventy-five percent of school funding is allocated based on age-weighted student numbers. Public schools cannot charge tuition fees. Schools are granted greater autonomy in management and administration and parents have free choice, although in practice competition is limited due to a rule that prevents the establishment of new schools as long as there are available places in public schools in the area. Only 5% of primary enrollments were in private schools in 2004.	Increase access and choice	The UK government, public and private schools
38	United States (Milwaukee and Florida)	Voucher scheme	The Targeted Voucher System in Milwaukee gave vouchers to kindergarten through 12th grade students from low-income families to enable them to attend accredited secular or religious private schools. Private schools must administer nationally recognized tests and cannot charge fees higher than the voucher amount, though they may charge for extra-curricular activities. The number of vouchers was capped at 22,500 in 2007 (up from 15,000 the previous year). The McKay Scholarships Program in Florida offers parents of special needs students who are dissatisfied with their children's existing schools the chance to transfer them to another public school. During the 2007–08 school year, the program provided 18,919 special needs students in Florida the opportunity to attend a participating private school. $119.1 million was paid to scholarship program participants in 2006–07.	Increase access and improve quality	School districts and private schools
39	United States (Puerto Rico)	Voucher scheme	This voucher program, which ended in 1995, was targeted to low-income families who could freely choose any school in any school district. The program covered 2,000 students in 1993 and over 14,000 in 1994. To qualify for a voucher, the student's family income had to be less than $18,000 per year. Any licensed or accredited school was entitled to receive vouchers.	Increase access and improve quality	The government of Puerto Rico, public and private schools
40	Venezuela, R. B. de	Venezuelan Association of Catholic Schools (AVEC)	The Ministry of Education and Culture gives subsidies to private schools located in low-income urban areas and indigenous communities, and to vocational schools and schools unable to meet more than 85% of their operational costs. While subsidies are nonconditional, schools must provide financial and management reports on an annual basis to government.	Increase access and improve quality	The Ministry of Education, Culture and Sports, AVEC, private schools under the AVEC network (some are Fe y Alegria schools)
			Supplemental and Support Services		
41	Australia	Tutorial Voucher Initiative	Parents and caregivers with children who score below a national reading benchmarking were eligible to receive a tutorial voucher valued up to $700. The voucher paid for a pre- and post-tuition assessment and a number of hours of reading tuition delivered one-to-one outside school hours. The initiative is administered by brokers who are responsible for contracting tutors, confirming student eligibility, providing parents/caregivers with a choice of tutors, and managing the initiative's administration. The initiative accounted for $20 million of government funding.	Improve quality and literacy skills	Brokers, private tutors, the federal government
42	Brazil	Pitagoras/ Corporate Sponsored Schools	The Pitagoras Network of Schools (PSN) works with a range of independent schools, most of which are private and charge tuition. Schools enter into a yearly contract with PSN, which then provides textbooks for all grades and students, teacher training services, and professional support. In return, schools have access to available services and are expected to participate in network activities.	Improve quality and increase efficiency in management	Independent schools, Pitagoras, corporations

	Country	Program	Program Description	Objective	Partners
			Supplemental and Support Services		
43	Colombia	Escuela Nueva Foundation	The Escuela Nueva Foundation delivers teacher training; designs curricula, textbooks, and educational materials; conducts research on pedagogical approaches; and advises governments on how to adapt the Escuela Nueva model in public schools. Escuela Nueva is a multi-grade rural school model that promotes leadership and cooperation between the administrative body, teachers, community, parents, and students.	Improve quality and provide technical assistance to schools and governments	The Ministry of Education, Fundacion Volvamos a la Gente, external funders, other national governments
44	India	Computer education in government schools	The NIIT, a global IT corporation, works with the state governments of Tamil Nadu, Karnataka, West Bengal, and Andhra Pradesh in infrastructure creation, systems integration, facilities management, education delivery, and teacher training, thereby providing quality computer education and computer-aided education to thousands of schools. Many of the classrooms have become NIIT centers, open to the school children and teachers during the day, then used by the franchise holder in the evenings.	Improve quality of computer education and computer-aided education and increase operational efficiency	NIIT, four state governments, government schools
45	Pakistan	Quality Advancement and Institutional Development in private schools	The Aga Khan Education Foundation provides a wide variety of school improvement programs including student-centered education, computers in the classroom, and preschool education. The objective of the program is to strengthen the capacity of low-cost private schools to improve the quality of the education delivered to poor communities.	Improve quality and increase efficiency	Aga Khan Education Services, the government, the Directorate of Private Education and Private Schools, private schools
46	Pakistan (Punjab)	Cluster-based Training of Teachers	The Cluster-based Training of Teachers program provides professional development for private school teachers with a focus on primary education. Training programs focus on developing teachers' knowledge of content rather than on pedagogical approaches. The training is provided to clusters of approximately 7 to10 schools and 30 to 35 teachers. Teachers are paid an allowance to attend the training that covers transportation and other costs. Training can be contracted out to the Punjab Education Foundation or to another private provider.	Improve quality	23 organizations, including 13 NGOs and private teacher training institutions, public schools, the Punjab Education Foundation
47	Pakistan (Sindh)	Quality Assurance Resource Center	The Sindh Education Foundation developed a quality assurance certification program to categorize schools in terms of their quality as a means of informing parents' schooling decisions. The program also provides tailored quality enhancement support for public, private, and community/NGO schools, including the training of teachers and school staff.	Improve quality	The Department of Education & Literacy, the government of Sindh, public, private, and community/NGO schools, the Sindh Education Foundation
48	United States	Supplemental educational services	Under the No Child Left Behind Act, private providers can be contracted to provide additional academic instruction in schools that have not made adequate yearly progress in increasing student achievement for three years. State education agencies identify organizations, whether public or private, that qualify to provide these services.	Improve quality and the academic achievement of low-performing students	State educational agencies, public and private schools, school districts, public and private providers
			Operational and Management Services		
49	Argentina	Fe y Alegria Network	Jesuit-controlled NGO that operates formal preschool, primary, secondary, and technical education (primarily formal primary education).	Improve quality of education provided to poor people	Ministries of Education, foundations, international agencies, civil society, communities
50	Bolivia	Fe y Alegria Network	Jesuit-controlled NGO that operates formal preschool, primary, secondary, and technical education (primarily formal primary education).	Improve quality of education provided to poor people	Ministries of Education, foundations, international agencies, civil society, communities

continued

	Country	Program	Program Description	Objective	Partners
	Operational and Management Services				
51	Brazil	Fe y Alegria Network	Jesuit-controlled NGO that operates formal preschool, primary, secondary, and technical education (primarily formal primary education).	Improve quality of education provided to poor people	Ministries of Education, foundations, international agencies, civil society, communities.
52	Canada (Alberta)	Charter schools	A small number of charter schools (capped at 15) operate in the province of Alberta in a similar manner to charter schools in the U.S. They have more management flexibility than public schools.	Improve quality and increase management efficiency and accountability	The Provincial government of Alberta, school boards, and private operators
53	Colombia	Concession schools	The management of public schools is turned over to private schools with proven track records of delivering high-quality education for a period of 15 years under performance-based contracts.	Improve quality and increase management, efficiency, and accountability	Secretaries of Education, associations of private educational providers
54	Colombia	Fe y Alegria Network	Jesuit-controlled NGO that operates formal preschool, primary, secondary, and technical education (primarily formal primary education).	Improve quality of education provided to poor people	Ministries of Education, foundations, international agencies, civil society, communities
55	Dominican Republic	Fe y Alegria Network	Jesuit-controlled NGO that operates formal preschool, primary, secondary, and technical education (primarily formal primary education).	Improve quality of education provided to poor people	Ministries of Education, foundations, international agencies, civil society, communities
56	Ecuador	Fe y Alegria Network	Jesuit-controlled NGO that operates formal preschool, primary, secondary, and technical education (primarily formal primary education).	Improve quality of education provided to poor people	Ministries of Education, foundations, international agencies, civil society, communities
57	El Salvador	Fe y Alegria Network	Jesuit-controlled NGO that operates formal preschool, primary, secondary, and technical education (primarily formal primary education).	Improve quality of education provided to poor people	Ministries of Education, foundations, international agencies, civil society, communities
58	Guatemala	Scholarships/ Eduque a la Nina	Vouchers were given to girls from low-income families to induce them to enroll in the first, second, and third grades of education. Implemented in 12 rural communities and involved approximately 800 girls over two years of age. The target communities were chosen because they had the greatest differences between male and female school attendance and graduation rates. Each girl's voucher was renewed conditional on the girl's promotion to the next grade.	Increase access and retention rates	Public schools, parent committees, teachers, and the Associacion Eduquemos a la Nina
59	Honduras	Fe y Alegria Network	Jesuit-controlled NGO that operates formal pre-school, primary, secondary, and technical education (primarily formal primary education).	Improve quality of education provided to poor people	Ministries of Education, foundations, international agencies, civil society, communities

	Country	Program	Program Description	Objective	Partners
			Operational and Management Services		
60	Nicaragua	Fe y Alegria Network	Jesuit-controlled NGO that operates formal pre-school, primary, secondary, and technical education (primarily formal primary education).	Improve quality of education provided to poor people	Ministries of Education, foundations, international agencies, civil society, communities
61	Pakistan	Adopt-a-School Program	Governments hand over control of under-utilized/failed schools to the NGO Itara-e-Taleem-o-Agahi (ITA), which takes them over and provides free schooling. ITA's role is to provide teacher training, formulate exercises, and make infrastructure improvements. ITA formulates a school council that is held responsible for monitoring and maintaining school facilities. A memorandum of understanding is formulated between ITA and the Department of Education, Punjab. No teachers or staff members are removed from their positions.	Improve quality of education	ITA and other civil society organizations, government schools, the Education Governorate
62	Pakistan	Pakistan Railways Schools	Pakistan Railways (PR) contracted Beaconhouse to operate schools for the children of their employees. School fees were minimal (PRs25) with an option to enroll students for a fee. Staffing decisions and hiring remained in the control of PR.	Improve school management	PR, Beaconhouse Schools
63	Pakistan	Management of Government Schools in Lahore City and Sarghoda	Cooperation for Advancement, Rehabilitation, and Education (CARE)—a local NGO—takes over the management of public schools by hiring internal, external, and academic coordinators who work with school staff; supervise the performance of CARE and government teachers; and monitor teacher attendance, performance, and test administration. CARE employs and pays 1,000 teachers (one-third) and the government employs 2000 (two-thirds). CARE also improves and provides additional infrastructure.	Improve management of schools and quality of education	CARE, public schools, government head teachers, academic coordinators, and internal and external coordinators to monitor school performance
64	Pakistan (Punjab)	Quality Education for All	The National Rural Support Program, a semi-autonomous not-for-profit agency, took over the management of 48 public schools through a 5-year contract with the district government. NRSP is responsible for the operational budget and maintenance and has authority over staff. The government remains responsible for capital works. The PPP is governed by a memorandum of understanding—a 5-year management contract—that sets out performance targets and accountabilities.	Improve quality of education in primary schools, reduce number of dropouts, and increase enrollments	National Rural Support Program, public schools, private sector, and district governments
65	Panama	Fe y Alegria Network	Jesuit-controlled NGO that operates formal pre-school, primary, secondary, and technical education (primarily formal primary education).	Improve quality of education provided to poor people	Ministries of Education, foundations, international agencies, civil society, communities
66	Paraguay	Fe y Alegria Network	Jesuit-controlled NGO that operates formal pre-school, primary, secondary, and technical education (primarily formal primary education).	Improve quality of education provided to poor people	Ministries of Education, foundations, international agencies, civil society, communities
67	Peru	Fe y Alegria Network	Jesuit-controlled NGO that operates formal pre-school, primary, secondary, and technical education (primarily formal primary education).	Improve quality of education provided to poor people	Ministries of Education, foundations, international agencies, civil society, communities

continued

	Country	Program	Program Description	Objective	Partners
			Operational and Management Services		
68	Qatar	Independent schools (IS)	ISs are government-funded (based on the number of students enrolled), privately managed schools. ISs can be newly established or existing public schools. Operators hire teachers and establish their own personnel policies. Contracts are for three years and are renewable conditional on school performance. Under the IS system, the government continues to assume the cost of education for eligible students and provides funds directly to the school. Operators can charge a fee to students who are not eligible for a subsidy. Operators are allowed to make a reasonable profit. Funding mechanisms include per pupil operating rate, start-up funding, and possible special grants.	Improve management of schools and quality of education and increase school independence	Private operators, the Supreme Education Council, the Ministry of Education of Qatar
69	United Kingdom	Education Action Zones	Local councils take bids from private organizations to run failing schools and to manage Education Action Zones (local clusters of 20 primary, secondary, and special schools). Education Action Zones were intended to run for an initial period of 3 years with the possibility of extending to 5 years, after which they should have been transformed into "Excellence Clusters."	Improve quality, tackle social exclusion, and promote innovation and greater cooperation between schools	Schools, local education authorities and other local organizations, the business community, higher education institutions
70	United Kingdom	Academies	Independent schools sponsored by businesses, faith-based groups, or voluntary groups working in partnership with the central government and local education partners. Funding comes from the Department for Education and Skills through a parity of funding with school operators. Private organizations become sponsors of academies and contribute up to £2 million towards their creation and are permitted to engage in trade in order to generate profits.	Improve quality and increase efficiency	Private enterprises, charities, philanthropists, the Department of Education and Skills
71	United States	Contract schools	Contract schools are privately managed but remain publicly owned and funded. Typically, private operators are brought in to manage the worst-performing schools. Students do not pay fees to attend these schools. Private sector operators must meet performance benchmarks and are paid a fixed amount per student, usually equivalent to the cost in the public sector, and a fixed management fee. Teaching and other staff continue to be employed by local authorities.	Improve quality and increase management efficiency and accountability	Local school boards, education management organizations, private educational providers
72	United States	Charter schools	Charter schools are publicly funded, privately run, secular public schools of choice that operate free from the regulations that apply to public schools. Charters are granted for three to five years. Schools must meet academic benchmarks and standards on curriculum and management or the contracts can be revoked. In 2007–08, there were over 4,000 charter schools, with enrollment rates of some 1.2 million.	Improve quality and increase management efficiency and accountability	District school boards, universities or other authorizing agencies in charge of granting charters (depending on local regulations). Managing agents include local communities, for-profit, and not-for-profit providers
73	Venezuela, R. B. de	Fe y Alegría Network	Jesuit-controlled NGO that operates formal preschool, primary, secondary, and technical education (primarily formal primary education). Fe y Alegría establishes schools for marginalized populations in urban areas and in isolated rural settings. FyA principals hire, train, and supervise teachers. The principal and the school council are at the center of local decision-making and the national government deals with strategic issues such as growth plans and fundraising. The government pays teacher and principal salaries, while external donors pay for land, construction, and maintenance of schools.	Improve quality of education provided to poor people	Ministries of Education, foundations, international agencies, civil society, communities

	Country	Program	Program Description	Objective	Partners
			Infrastructure Services/Education Services		
74	Australia	New Schools Project in New South Wales	The private sector finances, designs, and constructs public schools following standards established by the Department of Education and also provides cleaning, maintenance, repair, security, safety, utility, and related services for buildings, furniture, and equipment until 2032. Private operators receive performance-related monthly payments. At the end of the contract, the buildings will be transferred to the public sector.	Outsource and finance school construction and maintenance of infrastructure	Private operators, the State Department of Education and Training
75	Australia (South Australia)	Education Works New Schools	The private sector will deliver new school infrastructure. The funding arrangement provides for the development of six new schools in the Playford North, Inner North, and Inner West areas of metropolitan Adelaide. The project value is estimated at $128 million ($A134 million) for the 2006–07 budget	Outsource and finance school construction and maintenance of infrastructure	The government of South Australia, the Department of Education and Children
76	Australia (Queensland)	Private finance initiatives	The private sector will take responsibility for the construction and maintenance of seven schools over a 30-year contract, but the education services will still be provided by the government. The tasks to be contracted out to the private sector include building repairs, cleaning, janitorial duties, grounds-keeping, and security. Handing over responsibility for these services to the private sector will allow teachers to focus on providing education.	Outsource and finance school construction and maintenance of infrastructure	The Queensland State Government, private financial partners
77	Belgium (Flanders)	Private finance initiatives	The government selects a single consortium to be responsible for the design, construction, financing, and maintenance of all school building projects. The consortium does not own the buildings but will receive financial compensation over 30 years in exchange for making the buildings available to the schools. Secondary advantages include a decrease in costs due to economies of scale and the fact that school boards can focus on providing education.	Outsource and finance school construction and maintenance of infrastructure	The Flemish Agency for Infrastructure in Education, private financial partners
78	Canada	PPPs for Education Infrastructure Nova Scotia	The government contracts with private providers, on a basis of competitive bidding, the design, construction, finance, and maintenance of schools for a period of 20 years. Incentives were built into contracts to ensure quality construction and maintenance.	Outsource and finance school construction and maintenance of infrastructure	The government of Nova Scotia, private providers
79	Canada (Alberta)	Private finance initiatives	The Alberta Government is moving forward with the planning and construction of 14 new schools that will feature innovative design concepts for middle and senior high schools for the Calgary and Edmonton regions. These 14 new schools are part of a 20-year plan to build new schools in areas of greatest need.	Outsource and finance school construction and maintenance of infrastructure	The government of Alberta, construction firms, school jurisdictions, communities
80	Denmark	Trehoje School	A Design, Build, Maintain, and Operate contract for a period of 24 years valued at $24.5 million (DKr116 million)	Outsource and finance school construction and maintenance of infrastructure	Private operators and the government of Denmark
81	Egypt, Arab Rep. of	PPP for new schools	The government provides land while its private sector partners design, construct, finance, and furnish public schools and provide noneducational services under 15–20 year agreements.	Outsource and finance school construction and maintenance of infrastructure	The government of Egypt, private operators
82	Germany	Offenbach schools	The government contracts out the financing, refurbishment, and operation of government schools. Its private sector partners operate the schools for 15 years.	Outsource and finance school construction and maintenance of infrastructure	SKE, HOCHTIEF, the government of the County of Offenbach
83	Germany	City of Cologne schools	The government contracts out the refurbishment and operation of government schools. Its private sector partners operate schools for 15 years.	Outsource and finance school construction and maintenance of infrastructure	HOCHTIEF, the government of the City of Cologne

continued

	Country	Program	Program Description	Objective	Partners
			Infrastructure Services/Education Services		
84	Greece	Macedonia schools and Attica schools	Private operators will build 51 new schools using a Design, Build, Finance, Maintain, Operate mechanism valued at $424 million dollars (€269 million). Contracts are for periods of 25 years. The University of the Peloponnese is also being built under a PPP scheme.	Outsource and finance school construction and maintenance of infrastructure	Private operators and the government of Greece
85	India (Gujarat State)	Jointly financed schools	High school buildings are donated, built, and managed by local communities. The running expenses, including teacher salaries, are met by the government.	Outsource and finance school construction and maintenance of infrastructure	Local community in Gujarat State and government
86	Ireland	Design-build-operate- finance	The private sector consortium (Jarvis Project Limited) was contracted to design, build, operate, and finance five schools over a 25-year period. The first school was officially opened in 2002.	Outsource and finance school construction and maintenance of infrastructure	The Department of Education and Science, schools, the Jarvis Project Ltd
87	Korea, Republic of	Build-Transfer-Lease Scheme	The private sector finances and builds social infrastructure facilities, transfers ownership of the facilities to the government upon completion of the construction, is granted the right to operate the facilities for a specified period, and leases the facilities back to government in order to recover the project costs. Current plans are to use the BTL scheme for 973 schools and 51 universities with a value of $6.7 million dollars (W7 trillion).	Outsource and finance school construction and maintenance of infrastructure	Private operators and the government of Korea
88	Netherlands	Ypenburg suburb of the Hague	Government contracts with private operator to build and operate a new secondary school. The secondary school is expected to grow from 150 students at the beginning of the contract to 1,200 by 2009. The contract term is 30 years (1.5 years for construction and 28.5 years for maintenance, including cleaning, furniture, information, ICT, and possibly catering).	Outsource and finance school construction and maintenance of infrastructure	The TalentGroep consortium, the government of the Netherlands
89	Norway	Persbraten and Herbraten schools	Private sector operators build, maintain, and operate two schools for a period of 24 years. The transaction is valued at $100 million dollars (€64 million).	Outsource and finance school construction and maintenance of infrastructure	Private operators and the government of Norway
90	Pakistan	Leasing of public school buildings to private operators	The government leases under-used and dilapidated government school buildings to private schools. The private sector is given the right to operate a school in the afternoon shift, when the school building is closed. In exchange, the private operator must upgrade the building, pay the utility costs of both schools, contribute to the operating costs of both schools, and pay 10% of any profits to the public school council. More than 6,000 such schools are now operating in Punjab.	Lease public school buildings to private operators	Private operators, the Punjab government
91	Scotland	School estate strategy	The major capital investment in schools is made through public-private partnerships. The Scottish Executive has made commitments to build and refurbish schools.	Outsource and finance school construction and maintenance of infrastructure	The Scottish Executive, local authorities, private operators
92	United Kingdom	Private finance initiatives/ Building Schools for the Future	A capital project is designed, built, financed, and managed by a private sector consortium under a contract that typically lasts 30 years. The most common structure used is design-build-finance-operate. The private consortium is paid regularly from public money based on its performance throughout the contract period. If a consortium misses its performance targets, the payment is reduced. At the end of the contract period, the school is returned to the government.	Outsource and finance school construction and maintenance of infrastructure	Private operators, the Department of Children, Schools, and Families

appendix

B

Methods for Evaluation of Public-Private Partnership Programs and Policies in Basic and Secondary Education

Randomization and regression discontinuity regressions show the real magnitude of the effects of public-private partnership programs (the estimates are unbiased) under general assumptions. In general, randomized studies randomly assign people to treatment groups. For example, in the secondary school voucher program in Colombia, the number of people applying for the vouchers was larger than the number of places available. Since the program's budget allocation was not sufficient to cover the demand for vouchers, the recipients of the vouchers were selected using a lottery, creating a treatment group (those selected in the lottery) and a control group (those not selected in the lottery). The two groups had, on average, similar observable and unobservable characteristics.

Regression discontinuity analysis is typically applied when a program is allocated using a continuous variable. For instance, some programs use a means-tested index to select the target population. In this way, the program specifies that households that score below a certain cutoff point are eligible for the program and those above the cutoff point are not. In this case, the program's impact can be assessed by dividing individuals into a treatment group, containing individuals who score just below the cutoff point, and a control group, containing individuals who score just above the cutoff point. The two groups are assumed to have very similar characteristics, with the only difference between them being their inclusion or exclusion from the program. Intuitively, for individuals, the cutoff point is almost a random lottery. An important limitation of this method is that it can assess a program's impact on the population close to the cutoff point but not on the general population. In other words, it is a local estimator.

Instrumental variable and Heckman correction models produce correct, unbiased estimates under more stringent assumptions. Both methods require a variable with two traits. First, it must explain the decision of the school or student to participate in the program. Second, it cannot be correlated with any unobservable characteristic that explains the outcome of interest, such as test scores. This variable makes it possible to model participation in a program and, therefore, once self-selection is controlled for, it is possible to assess a program's impact. The difficulty with these two methods is finding a valid instrumental variable.

The difference in difference method compares beneficiaries and nonbeneficiaries before and after the program. Its key assumptions are that the trend in the outcome of interest before the intervention is equal for beneficiaries and nonbeneficiaries, and that all nonobservable variables that explain the outcome of interest are time-invariant.

Propensity score-matching estimators take a slightly different approach. This method assumes that program participation can be fully explained by a large array of observable characteristics measured at a baseline. Based on this information, the treatment and control groups are constructed and their outcome measures compared. The biggest challenge in using both difference in difference and propensity score-matching is obtaining the large array of baseline data needed to ensure the statistical similarity of the two groups.

References

Aedo, C. 1997. "Organización Industrial de la Prestación de Servicios Sociales." Working Paper Series R-302. Inter-American Development Bank, Washington, DC.

Aedo, C., and O. Larrañaga. 1994. "Educación Privada vs. Pública en Chile: Calidad y Sesgo de Selección." Graduate Economics Program, Santiago, and Instituto Latinoamericano de Doctrinas y Estudios Sociales Georgetown University, Washington, DC.

Ahlin, A. 2003. "Does School Competition Matter? Effects of a Large-Scale School Choice Reform on Student Performance." Department of Economics, Uppsala University, Sweden.

Allcott, H., and D. E. Ortega. 2007. "The Performance of Decentralized School Systems: Evidence from Fe y Alegría in Venezuela" Presented at the Conference on Public-Private Partnerships in Education, World Bank, Washington DC, June 7–8.

Andersen, S. C. 2005. "Selection and Competition Effects in a Large-Scale School Voucher System." For presentation at the conference European Public Choice Society 1005, University of Durham, United Kingdom, March 31 to 3 April.

———. "Private Schools and the Parents That Choose Them: Empirical Evidence from the Danish School Voucher System." *Scandinavian Political Studies* 31(1): 69.

Andrabi, T., J. Das, and A. I. Khwaja. 2006. "A Dime a Day: The Possibilities and Limits of Private Schooling in Pakistan." Policy Research Working Paper 4066. World Bank, Washington, DC.

Andrabi, T., J. Das, A. I. Khwaja, T. Vishwanath, and T. Zajonc. 2007. "Learning and Educational Achievements in Punjab Schools (Leaps): Insights to Inform the Education Policy Debate." World Bank, Washington, DC.

Angrist, J., E. Bettinger, E. Bloom, E. King, and M. Kremer. 2002. "Vouchers for Private Schooling in Colombia: Evidence from a Randomized Natural Experiment." *American Economic Review* 92(5): 1535–58.

Angrist, J., E. Bettinger, and M. Kremer. 2006. "Long-Term Educational Consequences of Secondary School Vouchers: Evidence from Administrative Records in Colombia." *American Economic Review* 96(3): 847–62.

Aslam, M. 2007. "The Relative Effectiveness of Government and Private Schools in Pakistan: Are Girls Worse Off?" RECOUP Working Paper 4. University of Cambridge, Cambridge.

Audit Office of New South Wales. 2006. "The New Schools Privately Financed Project." Sydney.

Baksh, Shaista. Forthcoming. "Public-Private Partnerships in World Bank Education Lending, 1998–2007: Background Report for the Role and Impact of Public-Private Partnerships in Education." World Bank, Washington, DC.

Barrera-Osorio, F. 2007. "The Impact of Private Provision of Public Education: Empirical Evidence from Bogota's Concession Schools." World Bank Policy Research Working Paper No. 4121, Washington, DC.

Barrera-Osorio, F., and H. A. Patrinos. 2009. "An International Perspective on School Vouchers" in *Handbook of Research on School Choice*, Peabody College at Vanderbilt University, Nashville, Tennessee.

Bedi, A. S., and A. Garg. 2000. "The Effectiveness of Private Versus Public Schools: The Case of Indonesia." *Journal of Development Economics* 69(2): 463–494.

Belfield, C. R., and A. L. Wooten. 2003. "Education Privatization: The Attitudes and Experiences of Superintendents." Occasional Paper 70. National Center for the Study of Privatization in Education, Columbia University, New York.

Bell, S. 1995 "Sharing the Wealth: Privatization through Broad-Based Ownership Strategies."

Discussion Paper 285. World Bank, Washington, DC.

Bellei, C. 2005. "The Private-Public School Controversy: The Case of Chile." Presented at the Conference on Mobilizing the Private Sector for Public Education, Harvard University, Cambridge, MA, October 5–6.

Benveniste, L. A., and P. J. McEwan. 2000. "Constraints to Implementing Educational Innovations: The Case of Multigrade Schools." *International Review of Education* 46(1–2): 31–48.

Bettinger, E. 2005. "The Effect of Charter Schools on Charter Students and Public Schools." *Economics of Education Review* 24 (2): 133–147.

Bettinger, E., M. Kremer, and J. E. Saavedra. 2008. "Are Vouchers Redistributive?" Mimeo Harvard, March 2008.

Bifulco, R., and H. F. Ladd. 2006. "The Impact of Charter Schools on Student Achievement: Evidence from North Carolina." *Journal of Education Finance and Policy* 1(1): 778–820.

Blomqvist, A., and E. Jimenez. 1989. "The Public Role in Private Post-Secondary Education: A Review of Issues and Options." Policy Research Working Paper 240. World Bank, Washington, DC.

Booker, K., S. M. Gilpatric, T. Gronberg, and D. Jansen. 2008. "The Effect of Charter Schools on Traditional Public School Students in Texas: Are Children who Stay Behind Left Behind?" *Journal of Urban Economics* 64(1): 123–145.

Borja, R. R. 2003. "China Seeking US Investment in Private School Sector." *Education Week* 24 September.

Bravo, D., D. Contreras, and C. Sanhueza. 1999. "Rendimiento Educacional, Desigualdad, y Brecha de Desempeño Privado Público: Chile 1982–1997." Department of Economy, University of Chile, Santiago.

Brewer, D., C. H. Augustine, G. L. Zellman, G. Ryan, C. A. Goldman, C. Stasz and L. Constant. 2007. "Education for a New Era. Design and Implementation of K–12 Education Reform in Qatar." RAND Corporation, Santa Monica, CA.

Burch, P., M. Steinberg, and J. Donovan. 2007. "Supplemental Educational Services and NCLB: Policy Assumptions, Market Practices, Emerging Issues." *Educational Evaluation and Policy Analysis* 29(2): 115–33.

Carnoy, M., R. Jacobsen, L. Michel, and R. Rothstein. 2005. *The Charter School Dust Up: Examining the Evidence on Enrollment and Achievement.* Economic Policy Institute, Washington, DC.

Carnoy, M., and P. McEwan. 2000. "The Effectiveness and Efficiency of Private Schools in Chile's Voucher System." *Educational Evaluation and Policy Analysis* 22(3): 213–39.

Carnoy, M., and P. J. McEwan. 2001. "Privatization through Vouchers in Developing Countries: The Cases of Chile and Colombia." In *Privatizing Education: Can the Marketplace Deliver Choice, Efficiency, Equity and Social Cohesion?*, ed. H. M. Levin, 151–177, Westview Press, United States.

Center for Education Reform. 2007. "National Charter School Data 2007–2008 New School Estimates." (http://www.edreform.com/ _upload/CER_charter_numbers.pdf).

Chakrabarti, R., and P. E. Peterson. 2008. *School Choice International: Exploring Public-Private Partnerships.* Cambridge, MA: MIT Press.

CIPPEC (Centro de Implementacion de Politicas Publicas para la Equidad y el Crecimiento. 2007. Programa de Monitoreo de la Ley de Financiamiento Educativo. Presentación No. 6. Aportes Financieros Estatales a la Educación Privada. Argentina.

Contreras, D., S. Bustos, and P Sepulveda. 2008. "When the Schools Are the Ones That Choose: Policy Analysis of the Screening in Chile." Department of Economy, University of Chile, Santiago.

Cox, D., and E. Jimenez. 1991. "The Relative Effectiveness of Private and Public Schools." *Journal of Development Economics* 34(1–2): 99–121.

Eggers, W. D. 1998. "Competitive Neutrality: Ensuring a Level Playing Field in Managed Competitions." How-to Guide No. 18, Reason Public Policy Institute, Los Angeles, CA.

Elacqua G., D. Contreras, and F. Salazar. 2008. "The Effectiveness of Private School Franchises In Chile's National Voucher Program." Paper presented at the World Bank Conference, "PrivatePublic Partnership," Washington, DC, June 7–8, 2007.

Epple, D., and R. E. Romano. 1998. "Competition between Private and Public Schools, Vouchers, and Peer-Group Effects" *American Economic Review*, 88(1): 33–62.

European Commission. 2007. "School Autonomy in Europe Policies and Measures." *Education and Culture DG.* Brussels, Eurydice.

Fielden, J., and N. LaRocque. 2008. "The Evolving Regulatory Context for Private Education in Emerging Economies". The World Bank Group International Colloquium on Private Education. Washington DC.

Filer, R. K., and D. Münich. 2000. "Responses of Private and Public Schools to Voucher Funding: The Czech and Hungarian Experience." William Davidson Institute Working Paper No. 360, University of Michigan, Ann Arbor.

Fiske, E. B., and H. F. Ladd. 2000. *When Schools Compete: A Cautionary Tale*. Washington, DC: Brookings Institution Press.

Fitz, J., and B. Beers. 2002. "Education Management Organizations and the Privatization of Public Education: A Cross-National Comparison of the USA and Britain." *Comparative Education* 38(2): 137–54.

Foundation Center. 2007. *Foundation Growth and Giving Estimates: Current Outlook*. New York: Foundation Center.

Friedman, M. 1955. "Role of Government in Education." In *Economics and the Public Interest,* ed. Robert Solo, 123–44. New Brunswick, NJ: Rutgers University Press.

Gallegos, F. 2004. "School Choice, Incentives, and Academic Outcomes: Evidence from Chile." Boston: MIT Press.

Gauri, V., and A. Vawda. 2004. "Vouchers for Basic Education in Developing Economies: A Principal Agent Perspective." World Bank Research Observer 19(2): 259–280.

Gibson, H., and B. Davies. 2008. "The Impact of Public Private Partnerships on Education." *International Journal of Education Management* 22(1): 74–89.

Gill, B. P., M. Timpane, K. E. Ross, D. J. Brewer, and K. Booker. 2007. *Rhetoric versus Reality: What We Know and What We Need to Know About Vouchers and Charter Schools*. Santa Monica, CA: RAND Education.

Government Accountability Office. 2006. "Education Actions Needed to Improve Local Implementation and State Evaluation of Supplemental Educational Services." Report to Congressional Requesters, Washington, DC.

Hanushek, E. A. 2003. "The Failure of Input-Based Schooling Policies." *Economic Journal* 113(485): F64–F98.

Hanushek, E. A., J. F. Kain, S. G. Rivkin, and G. F. Branch. 2007. "Charter School Quality and Parental Decision Making with School Choice" *Journal of Public Economics* 91(5–6): 823–848.

Hanushek, E. A., and L. Woessmann. 2007. *Education Quality and Economic Growth*. World Bank, Washington, DC.

Harding, A. L. 2002. "Introduction to the Private Participation in Health Services Handbook." In *Private Participation in Health Services Handbook*, eds. April L. Harding and Alexander S. Preker, 46 p. Washington, DC: World Bank.

Hatcher, R. 2003. "Privatization and the US School System: Voucher Programmes and Education Management Organisations." Paper presented at the ESRC Seminar, "Private Sector Participation in Public Sector Education," Institute of Education, London, 28 November, 2003.

———. 2006. "Privatization and Sponsorship: The Re-Agenting of the School System in England." *Journal of Education Policy* 21(5): 599–619.

Hentschke, G. C. 2005. "Characteristics of Growth in the Education Industry: Illustrations from U.S. Education Businesses." Discussion Draft, University of Bremen, Bremen.

Himmler, O. 2007. "The Effects of School Choice on Academic Achievement in the Netherlands." Georg-August-Universität Göttingen, Sweden.

HM Treasury. 2008. "Infrastructure Procurement: Delivering Long-Term Value." London.

House of Commons Education and Skills Committee. 2006–07. "Sustainable Schools: Are We Building Schools for the Future?" London.

Hoxby, C. M. 2000. "Does Competition among Public Schools Benefit Students and Taxpayers?" *American Economic Review* 90(5): 1209–38.

———, ed. 2003. *The Economics of School Choice*. Chicago: University of Chicago Press.

Hoxby, C. M., and S. Murarka. 2007. "Charter Schools in New York City: Who Enrolls and How They Affect Their Students' Achievements." National Bureau of Economic Research, Cambridge, MA.

Hoxby, C., and J. E. Rockoff. 2004. "The Impact of Charter Schools on Student Achievement." Taubman Center for State and Local Government, Kennedy School of Government, Cambridge, MA.

Hsieh, C. T., and M. Urquiola. 2006. "The Effects of Generalized School Choice on Achievement and Stratification: Evidence from Chile's Voucher Program." *Journal of Public Economics* 90(8–9): 1477–1503.

Hurst, C. 2004. "An Economic Analysis of Ireland's First Public Private Partnership." *International Journal of Public Sector Management* 17(5): 379–388.

IFC (International Finance Corporation). 2007. "IFC Supports Private Education in Africa." Media Release, 17 July. Washington, DC.

———. 2006. "Proposed Investment in School Financing & Technical Assistance Facility. Kenya". IFC/R2006-0278. World Bank. Washington DC.

IMF (International Monetary Fund). 2004. "Public-Private Partnerships." Fiscal Affairs Department (In consultation with other departments the World Bank and the Inter-American Development Bank). International Monetary Fund, Washington, DC.

International Financial Services London. 2001. "Public Private Partnerships: UK Expertise for International Markets." London.

———. 2008. "PFI in the UK and PPP in Europe 2008." IFSL Research. London.

Jallade, J. P. 1973. "The Financing of Education: An Examination of Basic Issues." Working Paper 157, World Bank, Washington, DC.

James, E. 1984. "Benefits and Costs of Privatized Public Services: Lessons from the Dutch Educational System." *Comparative Education Review* 28(4): 605–664.

——— 1993. "Why Do Different Countries Choose a Different Public-Private Mix of Educational Services?" *Journal of Human Resources* 28(3): 571–592.

Jones, D., B. Vann, and O. Hayford. 2004. "Public Private Partnerships—Managing the Challenges." Clayton Utz, Sydney, Australia.

Justesen, M. K. 2002. *Learning from Europe: The Dutch and Danish School Systems.* London: Adam Smith Institute.

Kang, C. 2007. "Classroom Peer Effects and Academic Achievement: Quasi-Randomized Evidence from South Korea." *Journal of Urban Economics* 61(3): 458–495.

Kim, J., H. Alderman, and P. F. Orazem. 1999. "Can Private School Subsidies Increase Enrollment for the Poor? The Quetta Urban Fellowship Program." *World Bank Economic Review* 13(3): 443–465.

Kingdon, G. 2007. "The Progress of School Education in India." *Oxford Review of Economic Policy* 23(2): 168–195.

KPMG. 2008. "Investment in School Facilities and PFI: Do They Play a Role in Educational Outcomes?" London.

Ladd, H. F. 2002. "School Vouchers: A Critical View." *Journal of Economic Perspectives* 16(4): 3–24.

———. 2003. "Comment on Caroline M. Hoxby: School Choice and School Competition: Evidence from the United States." *Swedish Economic Policy Review* 10: 67–76.

LaRocque, N. 1999. "The Private Education in Sector in West Africa: Overview Report." World Bank, Washington, DC.

———. 2002. *Private Education in the Philippines: A Market and Regulatory Survey.* Manila: Asian Development Bank.

———. 2008. "Public-Private Partnerships in Basic Education: An International Review" CfBT Education Trust, Berkshire.

LaRocque, N., and V. Jacobsen. 2000. "Private Education in Cameroon." World Bank, Washington, DC.

LaRocque, N. and H. Patrinos. 2006. "Choice and Contracting Mechanisms in the Education Sector." World Bank, Washington, DC.

Latham, M. 2005. "The PFI Model and its Effect on Educational Outcomes." Prepared for the conference Mobilizing the Private Sector for Public Education, 5–6 October, World Bank and Kennedy School of Government, Harvard University.

Levin, H. M. 2000. "The Public-Private Nexus in Education." In *Public-Private Policy Partnerships*, ed. P. Vaillancourt Rosenau, 129–142. Cambridge, MA: MIT Press.

Lewin, K. M., and Y. Sayed. 2005. "Non-Government Secondary Schooling in Sub-Saharan Africa. Exploring the Evidence in South Africa and Malawi." U.K. Department for International Development, London.

Lockheed, M., and W. van Eeghen. 1998. "Effective Financing of Education: Role of Public and Private Sectors." Paper presented at the 1998 Annual Seminar jointly organized by the Arab Monetary Fund and the Arab Fund for Economic and Social Development in collaboration with the International Monetary Fund and the World Bank, Abu Dhabi, February 21–22.

Loevinsohn, B., and A. Harding. 2005. "Buying Results? Contracting for Health Service Delivery in Developing Countries." *The Lancet* 366(9486): 676–681.

McEwan, P. 2001 "The Effectiveness of Public, Catholic, and Non-Religious Private Schools in Chile's Voucher System." *Education Economics* 9(2): 103–128.

McEwan, P. J., M. Urquiola, and E. Vegas. 2007. "School Choice, Stratification, and Student Performance: Lessons from Chile." *Economia. Journal of the Latin American and Caribbean Economic Association.* 8(2): 1–27.

Micklewright, J., and A. Wright. 2003. "Private Donations for International Development."

Discussion Paper 2003/82. United Nations University, World Institute for Development Economics Research, Helsinki.

Minnesota House of Representatives. 2003. "Charter Schools. Information Brief" Research Department. St. Paul. (http://www .house.leg.state.mn.us/hrd/pubs/chrtschl.pdf).

Mizala, A., and P. Romaguera. 2000. "School Performance and Choice: The Chilean Experience." *Journal of Human Resources* 35(2): 392–417.

Mohadeb, P., and D. Kulpoo. 2008. "The Provision and Financing of Quality Secondary Education. Through PPP in Mauritius. A Success Story." Working Document. Draft for *Beyond Primary Education: Challenges and Approaches to Expanding Learning Opportunities in Africa*. Association for the Development of Education in Africa.

Molnar, A., D. R. Garcia, M. Bartlett, and A. O'Neill. 2006. "Profiles of For-Profit Education Management Organizations." Arizona State University, Commercialism in Education Research Unit, Tempe.

Muralidharan, K., and M. Kremer. 2006. "Public and Private Schools in Rural India." Harvard University, Department of Economics, Cambridge, MA.

Nechyba, T. J. 2000. "Mobility, Targeting and Private School Vouchers." *American Economic Review* 90(1): 130–146.

The Netherlands Ministry of Education, Culture and Science. 2002. *Education, Culture and Science in the Netherlands, Facts and Figures 2002*.

OECD (Organisation for Economic Co-operation and Development). 2003. "Checklist for Foreign Direct Investment Incentive Policies." Paris. http://www.oecd.org/dataoecd/45/21/2506900 .pdf.

———. 2004a. "Australia's First Public Private Partnership School Project." *The Journal of the OECD Programme on Educational Building*. 2004/2. No. 52: 23.

———. 2004b. "The United Kingdom's Part-Privately Funded Business Academy Bexley." *The Journal of the OECD Programme on Educational Building* 52(2): 25.

———. 2006. "Public-Private Partnerships in Flanders." *PEB Exchange* 6 2006/6:1.

———. 2007a. "PISA 2006: Science Competencies for Tomorrow's World." Volume 1: Analysis, Paris.

———. 2007b. "Education at a Glance 2007." Paris.

Orazem, P. F. 2000. "The Urban and Rural Fellowship School Experiments in Pakistan. Design, Evaluation and Sustainability." The World Bank, Washington DC.

Palter, R. N., J. Walder, and S. Westlake. 2008. "How Investors Can Get More out of Infrastructure." *The McKinsey Quarterly* (February 2008).

Patrinos, H. A. 2000. "Market Forces in Education." *European Journal of Education* 35(1): 61–80.

———. 2002. "Private Education Provision and Public Finance: The Netherlands as a Possible Model." Occasional Paper No. 59, National Center for the Study of Privatization in Education, Teachers College, Columbia University.

———. 2005. "Education Contracting: Scope of Future Research." Program on Education Policy and Governance Report 05-23. Harvard University, Cambridge, MA.

Patrinos, H. A., and C. Sakellariou. 2008. "Quality of Schooling, Returns to Schooling and the 1981 Vouchers Reform in Chile." World Bank Policy Research Working Paper No. 5617, Washington, DC.

Patrinos, H. A., and S. Sosale. 2007. *Mobilizing the Private Sector for Public Education: A View from the Trenches*. Directions in Development: Human Development. Washington, DC: World Bank.

PricewaterhouseCoopers. 2005. "Delivering the PPP Promise: A Review of PPP Issues and Activity." Public Sector Research Centre. http://www.pwc.com/extweb/pwcpublications .nsf/docid/5D37E0E325CF5D71852570DC000 9C39B/$File/promisereport.pdf.

———. 2008. "The Value of PFI: Hanging in the Balance Sheet?" Public Sector Research Centre. http://www.ukmediacentre.pwc.com/ content/Detail.asp?ReleaseID=2617&NewsA reaID=2.

Raynor, J., and K. Wesson. 2006. "The Girls' Stipend Program in Bangladesh." Journal of Education for International Development 2:2. http://www.equip123.net/JEID/articles/3/ Girls'StipendPrograminBangladesh.pdf.

Rinne, R., J. Kivirauma, and H. Simola. 2002. "Shoots of Revisionist Education Policy or Just Slow Readjustment? The Finnish Case of Educational Reconstruction." *Journal of Education Policy* 17(6): 643–658.

Rodriguez, A., and K. Hovde. 2002. "The Challenge of School Autonomy: Supporting Principals." World Bank, Latin America and the Caribbean Regional Office, Washington, DC.

Rodriguez, J. 1988. "School Achievement and Decentralization Policy: The Chilean Case." *Revista de Análisis Económico* 3(1): 75–88.

Sadka, E. 2006. "Public-Private Partnerships: A Public Economics Perspective." IMF Working Paper WP/06/77. Washington, DC.

Sakellariou, C., and H. A. Patrinos. 2008. "Incidence Analysis of Public Support to the Private Sector in Côte d'Ivoire." *International Journal of Educational Development.*

Sandström, F. M., and F. Bergström. 2004. "School Vouchers In Practice: Competition Will Not Hurt You." *Journal of Public Economics* 89(2–3): 351–380.

Sapelli, C., and B. Vial. 2004. "Peer Effects and Relative Performance of Voucher Schools in Chile." Paper presented at the American Economic Association meetings, San Diego, CA, January 3.

Sarwar, M. B. 2006. "Documenting Educational Innovations. Sharing Practices for Educational Change." Sindh Education Foundation, Karachi.

Sass, T. R. 2005. "Charter Schools and Student Achievement in Florida." Working Paper. Florida State University, Tallahassee.

Savas, E. S. 2000. *Privatization and Public-Private Partnerships*, New York: Chatham House Publishers.

School Ventures. 2008. "The African Private Schools Investment Index (APSI) 2008." Washington, DC. http://www.schoolventures.com.

Schütz, G., M. R. West and L. Woessmann. 2007. "School Accountability, Autonomy, Choice and the Equity of Student Achievement: International Evidence from PISA." Education Working Paper No. 14. Directorate for Education, OECD, Paris.

Solmon, L. C. 2004. "Comparison of Traditional Public Schools and Charter Schools on Retention, School Switching, and Achievement Growth." Policy Report 192. Goldwater Institute, Phoenix, AZ.

Sosale, S. 2000. "Trends in Private Sector Development in World Bank Education Projects." Policy Research Working Paper 2452, World Bank, Washington, DC.

Srivastava, P. 2007. *Neither Voice nor Loyalty: School Choice and the Low-Fee Private Sector in India.* Occasional Paper 134, Research Publications Series, National Center for the Study of Privatization in Education, New York.

Tanzi, Vito, and Howell Zee. 2001. "Tax Policy for Developing Countries." Economic Issues 27. International Monetary Fund, Washington, DC.

Taylor, R. J. 2003. "Contracting for Health Services." In *Private Participation in Health Services Handbook*, eds. A. Harding and A. Preker, 195–204. Washington, DC: World Bank.

United Kingdom Audit Commission. 2003. "PFI in Schools: The Quality and Cost of Buildings and Services Provided by Early Private Finance Initiative Schemes." London.

United Nations Conference on Trade and Development (UNCTAD). Various Issues. *World Investment Report.* Geneva.

United Nations Educational, Scientific, and Cultural Organization (UNESCO). 2007. "Non-State Providers and Public-Private-Community Partnerships in Education." Background paper for the *Education for All Global Monitoring Report 2008: Education for All by 2015: Will We Make It?* A. K. F. Team. Paris.

United States Department of Education. 2007. "Improving Basic Programs Operated by Local Education Agencies (Title I, Part a)." Office of Elementary and Secondary Education, Washington, DC.

Uribe, C., R. Murnane, J. B. Willett, and M. Somers. 2006. "Expanding School Enrollment by Subsidizing Private Schools: Lessons from Bogotá." *Comparative Education Review* 50(2): 241–277.

Vegas, E. 2002. "School Choice, Student Performance, and Teacher and Student Characteristics: The Chilean Case." Policy Research Working Paper 2833, World Bank, Washington, DC.

Verspoor, A. M. 2008. "The Power of Public-Private Partnership: Coming Together for Secondary Education in Africa." Working Document Draft, Association for the Development of Education in Africa, Paris.

VietNamNet Bridge. 2006. "City's Education Sector Gets Four More FDI Projects." August 24. http://english.vietnamnet.vn/biz/2006/08/605411/.

Villa, L. and J. Duarte. 2005. "Concessionary Public Schools in Bogota." In *Private Education and Public Policy in Latin America*, eds. L. Wolff, J. C. Navarro, and P. Gonzales, 95–130. Washington, DC: PREAL.

Wang, Y. 2000. *Public-Private Partnerships in the Social Sector. Issues and Country Experiences in Asia and the Pacific.* Tokyo: Asian Development Bank Institute.

World Bank. 2003a. *World Development Report 2004: Making Services Work for Poor People.* Washington, DC.

———. 2003b. *Partnerships within the Public Sector to Achieve Health Objectives.* Washington, DC.

———. 2003c. "Project Performance Assessment Report" Bangladesh, Female Secondary School Assistance Project. Sector and Thematic Evaluation Group, Operations Evaluation Department. Report 26226. Washington, DC.

———. 2004. *Public Communication Programs for Privatization Projects—A Toolkit for World Bank Task Team Leaders and Clients.* Washington, DC: Development Communications Unit, External Affairs Vice Presidency.

———. 2006. "Colombia Contracting Education Services." Report 31841-CO. Washington, DC.

———. 2007a. *What Is School-Based Management?* Human Development Network, Washington, DC.

———. 2007b. "Haiti Education For All Adaptable Program Grant" Human Development Sector, Latin America and Caribbean Region. Report 38600, Washington, DC.

———. 2008. "Performance-Based Contracting for Health Services in Developing Countries. A Toolkit." World Bank Institute, Health, Nutrition and Population Series. Washington, DC.

World Bank Education Statistics Version 5.3. 2008. Washington, DC. http://www.worldbank.org/education/edstats.

Woessmann, L. 2005. "Public-Private Partnerships in Schooling: Cross-Country Evidence on their Effectiveness in Providing Cognitive Skills." Prepared for the conference Mobilizing the Private Sector for Public Education, World Bank and Kennedy School of Government, Harvard University, Cambridge, MA, October 5–6.

Yilmaz, Yesim. 1998. *Private Regulation: A Real Alternative for Regulatory Reform.* Cato Report No. 303, Cato Institute, Washington, DC.

Index

Boxes, figures, and tables are indicated by *b, f,* and *t,* respectively.